You are already perceiving.

This book is where noticing begins.

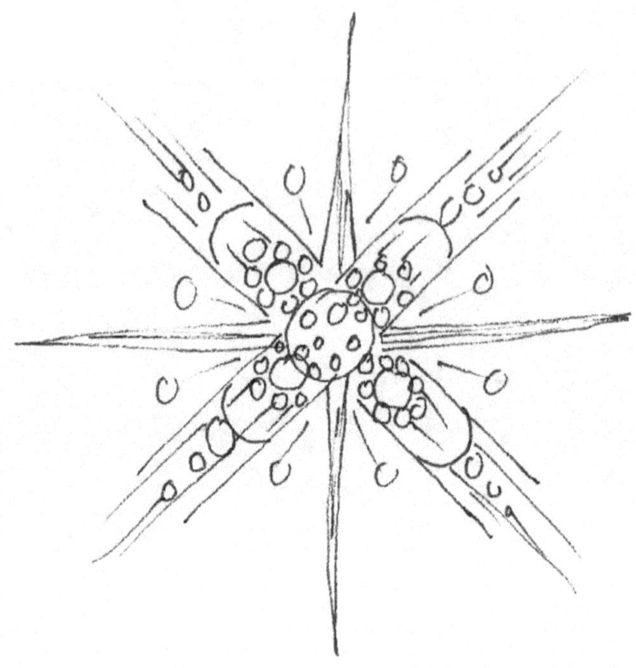

You Know More Than You Think
A Five-Book Series

Book One
What's Already There
Explorations in Noticing

Elly Flippen

A BIOMIND SUPERPOWERS BOOK
PUBLISHED BY

Swann-Ryder Productions, LLC

DISCLAIMER

This book is provided for informational, educational, and experiential purposes only. It is not intended as medical, psychological, psychiatric, therapeutic, legal, or scientific advice, nor should it be used as a substitute for professional diagnosis, treatment, or consultation.

The author is affiliated with Swann-Ryder Productions, LLC, which holds certain copyrights and related intellectual property rights to the published and unpublished writings and artwork of Ingo Swann. This book may reference, quote, or discuss his published material for educational and contextual purposes. All interpretations, analyses, applications, and contemporary extensions presented herein are solely those of the author.

Nothing in this book should be interpreted as representing official positions of any scientific, governmental, institutional, or research organization. References to perception research, anomalous experience, or non-ordinary awareness are included for historical, educational, and phenomenological exploration.

This work does not claim to prove, validate, or guarantee the existence of paranormal, psychic, extrasensory, or supernatural abilities, nor does it present such phenomena as scientifically established fact.

Individual experiences will vary. No guarantees are made regarding outcomes, results, insights, or personal transformation.

Readers are responsible for their own engagement with the material and for their physical, emotional, and psychological well-being. Individuals with a history of trauma, dissociation, significant mental health conditions, neurological or cardiovascular concerns, or other medical conditions should consult a qualified healthcare professional before engaging in any practices described.

The practices described in this book are voluntary exercises intended for personal exploration and should be approached with discretion and self-awareness.

While reasonable efforts have been made to ensure the accuracy of the information presented, the author and Swann-Ryder Productions, LLC assume no responsibility for errors or omissions and make no warranties regarding the completeness, reliability, or applicability of the material.

By choosing to engage with this book, the reader accepts responsibility for its use and for any decisions or actions arising from the material presented.

READER GUIDANCE

The following guidance is offered to support safe, grounded, and thoughtful engagement with the practices and explorations presented in this book.

Readers are encouraged to:

- Move at a pace that feels appropriate and sustainable.
- Modify, pause, or discontinue any practice that creates discomfort, distress, or instability.
- Seek qualified professional support when encountering intense emotional, psychological, or perceptual experiences.

The material in this book is not intended to replace sound judgment, professional care, or responsible engagement with daily life, relationships, and decision-making.

These practices are offered as invitations to explore awareness and perceptual literacy, not as doctrines of belief, systems of authority, or substitutes for medical, psychological, or therapeutic care.

Your consent, grounding, safety, and discernment are foundational to your engagement with the material presented here.

TABLE OF CONTENTS

AUTHOR'S BEGINNING NOTE

Note on Perspective

Before opening this series, it feels important to acknowledge a quiet reminder: perception does not expand outward first, but inward.

What we call the infinite does not begin in abstraction, but in the moment attention returns to lived sensation, the place where fear loosens its grip and curiosity re-emerges as wonder.

Turning inward in this way is not withdrawal. It is engagement. It is the point at which sensation, emotion, and attention begin to organize in ways that reinforce one another rather than compete.

It is where responses arise from discernment instead of reflex.

The five volumes are for those who have sensed more than they were encouraged to trust, and who are willing to examine that sensing carefully, physiologically, and without exaggeration.

To do so requires looking beneath behavior to the processes that precede it: before behavior there is motion, before motion there is vibration, and before vibration there is a living intelligence within the human being.

It is an embodied system that detects and responds long before the mind intervenes to explain. This work refers to that capacity as *organismic intelligence*.

The framework presented here draws from predictive processing (the idea that the brain continually predicts and updates its model of the world), interoception research (how we sense our body's internal state), affective neuroscience (the study of emotion and feeling in the brain and body), and contemporary cognitive science (the interdisciplinary study of mind and perception).

It offers a descriptive model of perception and regulation, not a metaphysical claim. Its purpose is not to explain experience away, but to invite a grounded encounter with it: a practical framework for direct self-experiencing.

Modern science is very good at measuring what bodies do. It observes outcomes and names them behavior. What it often overlooks is the deeper architecture beneath those outcomes: a quiet, continuous mode of awareness through which the body senses, organizes, and responds before behavior becomes visible.

A human being is not a machine assembled from habits, but a living organism… an instrument of perception.

The word *organ* once meant instrument: something that resonates. In that older sense, the body is exactly that: a responsive system of cells, nerves, and rhythms, continually attuning to its environment. It vibrates not metaphorically, but functionally, as all living systems do.

Understanding this is vital, because perception does not occur outside the body; it arises through the living instrument we are. To understand perception, then, we must also understand vitality itself.

The word *vital* once referred not merely to vigor, but to life as principle: the animating current moving through living systems. To be alive is to be shaped and stirred by that current, whether one is consciously aware of it or not.

What we experience as emotion, creativity, sexuality, presence (what people casually call "vibes") and knowing itself are not separate faculties to be examined in isolation.

They are expressions of a single underlying process: organismic intelligence unfolding through the body as lived experience.

Behavior is the surface, motion is the bridge, vibration is the signal, and organismic intelligence is the source beneath them all.

What has often been dismissed as intuition, instinct, or anomaly may in fact reflect this deeper architecture of sensing. The organism is not waiting for belief to activate it. It is already receiving, sorting, predicting, and responding. The question is not whether perception is occurring, but whether attention is refined enough to recognize it.

Long before contemporary cognitive science began revising the "five-senses" model of perception, researchers were already documenting that human beings possess far more complex receptor systems than cultural narratives allowed.

Ingo Swann, a researcher of human perception and my uncle, presented a 1994 lecture at the United Nations titled *"New Scientific Discoveries Regarding the Existence of Certain Psi Faculties."* In it, he drew attention to emerging biological research suggesting that subtle forms of perception may be rooted in measurable receptor systems: electrochemical, electromagnetic, and neural networks continuously exchanging information within and across the organism.

He pointed readers toward works such as *Sensation and Perception: An Integrated Approach* by H.R. Schiffman and *Deciphering the Senses: The Expanding World of Human Perception* by Robert Rivlin and Karen Gravelle, texts that explored the expanding scientific understanding of human sensory systems and challenged the simplicity of the five-sense framework.

Whatever terminology one prefers, the implication is apparent: the human being is not limited to a narrow sensory bandwidth.

It is an array of living receptors (chemical, neural, and electromagnetic) in continuous dialogue with its environment.

This series does not attempt to settle debates about anomalous perception, nor does it lean on metaphysical claims.

Instead, it returns to something simpler and more immediate: the fact that your body is already sensing, already predicting, already organizing experience before conscious narrative forms.

You are not separate from that source.

You are composed of it, moved by it, and sensing through it at every moment of your life.

This series does not aim to add anything new. It is concerned instead with recognizing what has always been active beneath conscious awareness: direct perception, resourceful intelligence, and the attention-based sensitivity your body has carried since birth.

You are the instrument, whether you have been taught to listen or not.

I owe the return to that perspective to filmmaker Fabian Rush, whose presence helped re-anchor this work in experience rather than explanation, and in trust rather than effort.

May this series serve as a remembering, not of something mystical, but of something immediate. Not an expansion outward, but a quiet turn inward, toward the organismic intelligence that has been sensing all along.

Consciousness Spectrum

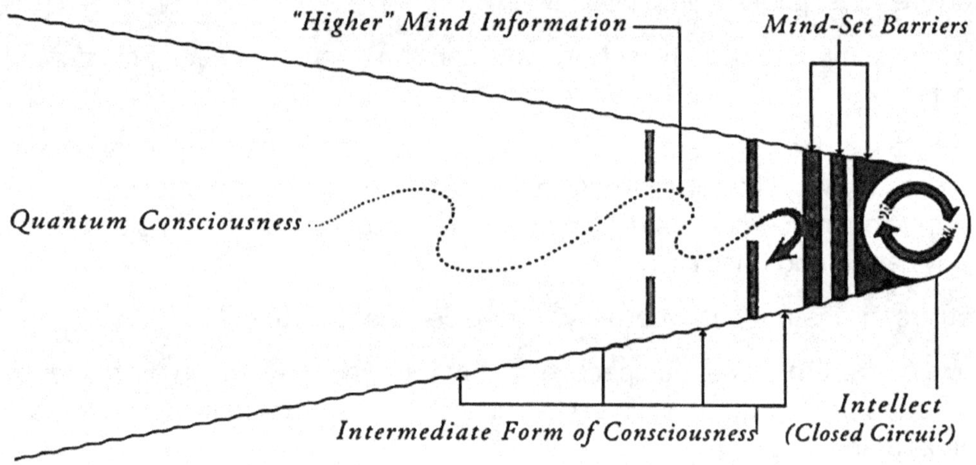

Carrying the Thread Forward

For most of my young adulthood, I watched Ingo attempt to describe something that resists easy explanation: the way human perception actually operates beneath the simplified models we are taught.

Best known as a pioneer of the United States intelligence community's remote viewing research, Ingo developed structured perceptual protocols in the 1970s at Stanford Research Institute (SRI) designed to explore whether distant targets could be perceived under controlled conditions. What he was pointing toward, however, was not an anomaly or a belief system, but a level of sensory and informational processing that biology is only beginning to learn how to describe.

He drew diagrams (circles, fields, channels, thresholds, comparators, roots, signals) not to explain perception away, but to work with it directly, stripped of myth and ornament.

In his early years, after immersing himself in the vast literatures of mysticism and the occult, Ingo came to recognize both their allure and their danger. Those traditions had preserved fragments of genuine perceptual insight, he felt, but they lacked, he thought, the biological framing and experimental grounding needed to distinguish raw data from projection.

They pointed, he noted, toward a crucial insight, that human awareness extends beyond the limits of the classically defined five physical senses.

Yet they were crowded with fantasy, projection, and symbolic excess.

Over time, he became acutely aware of how easily genuine perceptual capacities could be obscured by these overlays, and how magic, once invoked, tended to replace inquiry.

The diagrams became his answer: a disciplined attempt to engage perception itself at the level where biological sensing, signal integration, and meaning formation converge, without mystification and without losing the wonder that had first drawn him in.

His schemata were never intended as mystical symbols or definitive maps, but as practical models, visual tools supporting inquiry and function.

Through them, small portions of perception's otherwise hidden organization could become momentarily visible, without mistaking the map for the living process itself.

Some of these diagrams appeared in his published books, including *Everybody's Guide to Natural ESP* and *Your Nostradamus Factor*. Others remained private for decades, preserved in folders, sketchpads, and personal notes that now reside in the Ingo Swann Papers at the University of West Georgia.

Together they reveal deeper layers of his thinking: attempts to trace symbolic processing, dimensional signal pathways, unconscious filtering, the geometry of awareness, and the early formation of knowing impressions long before they rise into conscious thought.

Taken together, the illustrations form a kind of internal atlas of the human perceptual system before culture narrows it.

It is easy to assume that these diagrams point toward paranormal or esoteric ideas. But to sit with Ingo, to hear the way he spoke about perception, was to recognize something far more universal: a natural sensory intelligence (what I refer to here as *organismic intelligence*) that every human being already possesses, and through which information is integrated, prioritized, and acted upon.

To make sense of how perception actually operates, Ingo drew a sharp distinction not only between different modes of perception, but between different states of awareness.

He observed that perception typically functions when awareness is largely passive (organized by habit, expectation, and learned interpretation) and that it can function differently when awareness is active and receptive, allowing the system to encode information more directly.

He described these two modes as indirect perception and direct perception.

Indirect perception refers to awareness that is mediated through sensory input and then intellectually filtered through learned categories, definitions, and conceptual frameworks. In this mode, perception relies on the classical senses and is processed, compared, and organized by established cognitive pathways.

This is the form of perception most commonly understood as ordinary awareness. It is effective, communicable, and necessary for navigating daily life, yet constrained by what existing concepts are able to recognize and name.

Direct perception, referred to in this book as *organismic perception*, describes perception when awareness is actively receptive rather than passively organized.

Organismic perception is the body's capacity to register information prior to conceptual interpretation. It does not rely on the classical sensory channels alone yet remains grounded in the body's distributed sensing systems and neural integration processes.

Through this mode, the system discerns shifts in pattern, relevance, and coherence (the degree to which incoming information fits, aligns, or resonates across a person's internal state, environmental context, and ongoing activity) before those registrations are translated into language or deliberate thought.

He often illustrated this distinction with a simple example: When a person dreams, they may recall images with clarity and detail even though their eyes were closed and their body asleep.

The experience of seeing occurred without the use of the eyes. Something in the human system perceived directly and delivered a result comparable to vision. From this, Ingo concluded that human awareness includes a capacity to become aware of information without passing through conventional sensory routes.

In everyday vernacular, people already recognize this capacity. They say things like "I knew it deep down," "I just had a feeling," "something in my gut told me," or "I had a bad feeling about it." Others remark that "something didn't sit right," that their "instincts kicked in," or that they could "feel it in their bones." Still others describe moments when "my heart sank," "I got chills," or "the hair on the back of my neck stood up." These expressions are not merely figures of speech. They point to a form of knowing that is often registered in the body before it is articulated in thought.

What people are pointing to in these moments is commonly labeled intuition. Yet intuition, as it is usually understood, is not a sudden idea, a guess, or an abstract insight. It is a felt registration. It is an internal orientation that arrives through sensation, tone, or bodily response before it takes the form of words, images, or conclusions.

This is why intuition is so often associated with the body, especially the gut. This form of perception is detected first as felt indication rather than narrative. The body senses pattern and direction (a felt sense) before conscious reasoning (what Ingo called the *intellect*) assembles explanation. What arrives initially is not a conclusion, but a sense of coherence or dissonance.

In this work, that capacity is not referred to as intuition, a term burdened with ambiguity and cultural misunderstanding. Instead, it is described as inferential knowing: one's innate ability to assemble pattern, relevance, and directional meaning prior to conscious reasoning taking over.

Inferential knowing does not bypass the reasoning. It precedes it. It provides pre-conceptual information that conscious thought, the intellect, may later analyze, interpret, or ignore. When this early *insight* is overridden, people often say they "knew all along" only in *hindsight*. When it is recognized early, decision-making tends to feel clearer, steadier, and less effortful.

Inferential knowing is not a special faculty or mysterious gift. It is the felt expression of organismic perception as it infers, organizes, and responds before conscious thought forms... what we might call the felt-senses.

From a biological perspective, this involves information registered through distributed sensory and regulatory systems (somatic, emotional, relational, and environmental) rapidly integrated into a coherent orientation before conscious reasoning engages. This information feels immediate not because it is unstructured, but because its organizing work has already been completed outside passive awareness.

This is why "just knowing" often proves reliable in familiar or high-stakes situations such as skilled performance, caregiving, navigation, or social attunement. In these contexts, organismic perception has been repeatedly calibrated through experience, allowing inferential knowing to operate with speed and coherence.

Where calibration is poor, or overwhelmed by fear, expectation, or internal noise, this information becomes unreliable. This occurs not because it is irrational, but because the underlying perceptual signals are disordered or misread.

Seen this way, this pathway is neither a mystical power nor a mental shortcut. It is the stage at which information has registered but has not yet become articulated thought. It is the experiential trace of organismic intelligence at work.

What is often dismissed as emotional response is better understood as perception operating in its original sense of the word. Sense comes from the Latin *sentīre*: to feel, perceive, and absorb. In this older understanding, meaning was not produced by cognition alone but emerged from one's direct engagement with the environment. Thought followed perception; explanation followed registration.

In this light, organismic perception is not a departure from reason, but its biological precursor.

This understanding was once commonplace.

In Roman thought, the *sensorium* referred not to a purely mental abstraction but to the embodied seat of perception, the capacity through which a person notices presence, tone, and influence as sensory experience.

Greek philosophers used the term *aisthēsis* to describe perception as sensory knowing. It was thought of as the immediate, embodied awareness through which the world becomes present to us.

Similar understandings appear across ancient cultures.

Early Hebrew texts locate discernment in the *lev* (heart), understood as the inner core of the person: the center of thought, will, moral understanding, and orientation toward meaning. Classical Chinese philosophy described *xin* (heart-mind) as the integrated center of perception, feeling, and moral attunement rather than a purely cognitive faculty.

In early Indian philosophy, *pratyakṣa* referred to direct perceptual knowledge, distinguished from inference and conceptual reasoning. While in ancient Egyptian thought the *ib* (heart) functioned as the center of perception, intention, and moral orientation. It was the locus in which truth was recognized and one's life aligned with *Ma'at*, the principle of cosmic order and harmonious balance that structured both the universe and ethical life.

Across these traditions, perception was understood as holistic and pre-reflective. It was an integrated, organismic registration of reality that occurred before analysis, judgment, or conceptual division. These were not transcendent abstractions, but descriptions of lived experience.

As such, awareness was not seen as something that observed the world from a distance, but as something already participating in it, registering meaning, orientation, and relevance prior to reflective thought. Only later did Western culture narrow perception into something assumed to occur primarily "in the head."

As philosophical and scientific traditions increasingly emphasized abstraction, categorization, and symbolic reasoning, perception came to be treated as a mental event rather than an organismic one.

Sensation was separated from meaning, the body reduced to a delivery system for sensory data, and awareness progressively relocated into cognition alone, where *sense* came to mean primarily logical intelligibility. More directly, what could be explained, justified, or "made sense of." This shift was reinforced by early models of neuroscience and psychology that focused on localized brain function and linear stimulus–response pathways. What could be measured reliably (neural firing, sensory thresholds, reaction times) came to define what was considered real and, by extension, what was treated as *sensible*.

Forms of perception that were distributed, preconscious, or resistant to experimental isolation were often set aside. Not because they failed under scrutiny, but because the instruments of scrutiny were still evolving.

Modern neuroscience, however, has quietly begun to return to earlier insights by expanding its scope, not by abandoning rigor. Advances in physiology, systems neuroscience, and complexity theory now reveal perception as a whole-body process unfolding across neural, hormonal, electromagnetic, and regulatory systems.

Research into interoception, neuropeptide signaling, bioelectromagnetic sensitivity, and predictive processing shows that the body continuously integrates information long before conscious interpretation begins, through internal sensation, chemical signaling, anticipatory responsiveness, and pattern recognition operating beneath awareness.

Taken together, these lines of research describe perception not as something confined to the brain, but as an embodied, distributed process: a perceptual awareness system spanning brain, body, and environment, one that operates prior to deliberate reflection and continually shapes it.

Meaning is not added afterward by cognition alone; it emerges from ongoing organismic activity that patterns experience before reflective awareness names it.

In this light, contemporary science does not overturn earlier understandings of perception so much as corroborate them, translating philosophical insight into biological evidence.

What has changed is our capacity to observe and describe it with greater precision rather than the nature of perception itself.

Organismic perception, then, is neither new nor extraordinary. It is the continuation of an ancient organismic intelligence that has always preceded language, logic, and deliberate thought. From this perspective, Ingo understood human perception as operating through three interdependent capacities:

⟩ One capacity evaluates and structures experience, comparing inputs, sorting distinctions, and building coherent understanding once information has entered conscious awareness.
⟩ Another capacity registers experience directly through the body and emotional frequencies / tones, tracking shifts in internal state, relational

atmosphere, and environmental texture, allowing one's system to orient and respond before deliberate thought occurs.

⟩ A third capacity apprehends patterns immediately, recognizing coherence, direction, or significance without step-by-step reasoning.

None of these functions is superior to the others; perception becomes reliable only when they operate together.

What are often labeled as special forms of awareness are not exceptional abilities, but baseline functions of perception operating beneath conscious thought.

What people experience as knowing is the felt presence of perception recognizing coherence before analysis begins. It is pattern recognition occurring prior to explanation.

Ingo believed we are instruments of perception, designed to resonate with our environment, with one another, and with dimensions of information that do not originate solely in what is immediately visible or physically present. Cognition follows sensation, not the other way around.

In this light, his diagrams were never meant as rigid explanations; they were invitations to look more carefully.

From Inquiry to Experience

In an earlier book I edited, *Why Do We Feel There Is More to Us Than We, or Anyone, Knows About?*, I explored these questions through Ingo's cultural, philosophical, and historical vantage point, working directly with his essays from his *Superpowers of the Human Biomind* archive.

That work examined how awareness and perception have been marginalized, and how social and institutional forces shape which forms of knowing are encouraged, tolerated, or suppressed. It asked why human beings sense more than they are taught to recognize.

This book begins where that inquiry necessarily concluded.

Rather than arguing for expanded perception, the focus here is on how perception appears as bodily sensation, emotional tone, and attentional orientation before it is shaped by interpretation, metaphor, or ideology.

The emphasis is not on extraordinariness, rather it is on literacy: experiencing how to notice, stabilize, interpret, and live with perceptual information in a grounded and coherent way.

This includes examining how information that is not immediately available through the five-named physical senses is nevertheless detected by the human system, not visually or theatrically, but somatically, emotionally, innately, and symbolically. Most often, it appears as understated shifts in atmosphere, timing, resonance, or felt knowing rather than as dramatic imagery.

Instead of grounding this inquiry in speculative physics or metaphysical claims, this work begins with a simpler observation: human experience routinely exceeds what current explanatory models can comfortably account for.

Across cultures, professions, and historical periods, there exists a vast body of consistent testimony describing moments of knowing or recognition that arise without evident sensory or inferential pathways.

These accounts do not constitute proof of a particular theory, but they do point to the limits of our present frameworks for understanding perception.

The gap, then, is not between belief and science, but between lived experience and explanation.

This series approaches that gap not by attempting to resolve it conceptually, but by examining how such experiences take shape within the human system itself, before interpretation or belief organize them.

Seen together, the two works form a single arc: from questioning what has been overlooked to experiencing how to inhabit perception responsibly.

Echoes of Ingo's diagrams appear throughout the series' chapters, not because I attempted to reproduce his models, but because many of the insights he carried now live in me in a more embodied form.

His work provides the lineage beneath this one, even as the framework evolves for a contemporary reader.

This is not a reinterpretation of his diagrams. It is a translation of the animating intelligence behind them: the understanding that perception extends beyond eyesight, awareness beyond attention, and distance is not the primary constraint on what human perception can take in when the system is coherent.

This series is offered in respect for the legacy he left behind, and in the hope that it invites you to notice capacities you already use, often unconsciously: sensitivity to subtle cues, pattern recognition beneath thought, the sensing of presence and absence beyond immediate contact, and an awareness that clarifies when it is not forced.

Ingo's diagrams pointed to the path. Your perception will walk it.

HOW TO APPROACH THIS SERIES

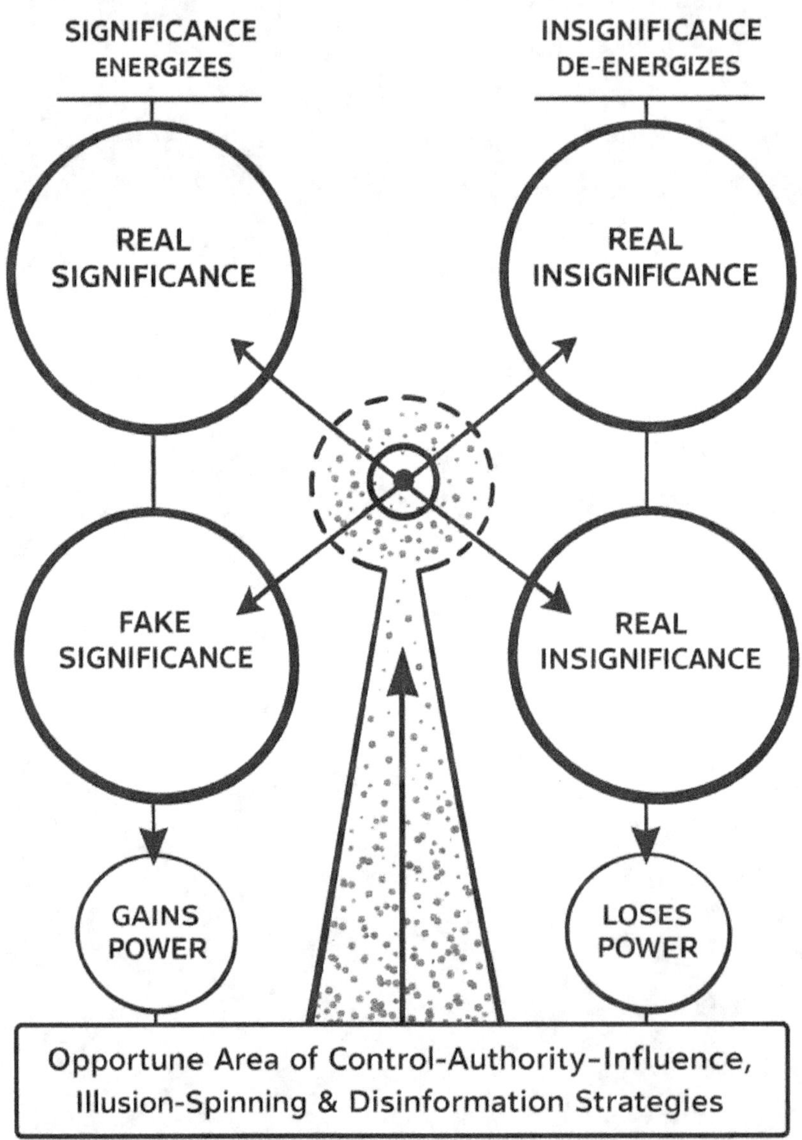

HUMAN CONSENSUS-THINK DETERMINES
SIGNIFICANCE & INSIGNIFICANCE
WHETHER REAL OR IMAGINED

SIGNIFICANCE
ENERGIZES

INSIGNIFICANCE
DE-ENERGIZES

REAL
SIGNIFICANCE

REAL
INSIGNIFICANCE

FAKE
SIGNIFICANCE

REAL
INSIGNIFICANCE

GAINS
POWER

LOSES
POWER

Opportune Area of Control-Authority-Influence,
Illusion-Spinning & Disinformation Strategies

The Value of First-Hand Experience

This series is structured around direct experience for a reason.

> Concepts can orient attention.
> Language can clarify distinctions.
> Diagrams can make organization visible.

But none of these, on their own, reorganize perception. Only first-hand experience does that. Second-hand knowledge is different.

Ingo consistently emphasized that second-hand knowledge, no matter how compelling, always arrives through filters. What is passed along is not perception itself, but interpretation shaped by the limits of someone else's awareness.

Because of this, second-hand information (ideas, explanations, interpretations) can be absorbed without altering how you actually perceive. You may agree with it, disagree with it, find it interesting, or reject it. But your perceptual patterns often remain intact.

First-hand experience unfolds another way.

When you notice something directly (a shift in tone, a boundary tightening—the body's sense of where something begins, ends, or changes in relation—or a symbolic fragment arising before interpretation), the parameters of your perception adjust. Attention reorganizes. What was previously fused begins to separate. This reorganization cannot be installed from the outside. It emerges from within your own perceptual system..

For this reason, the series does not begin with belief, theory, or persuasion. It begins with noticing.

Understanding here is cumulative. Each direct experience builds upon the last, gradually expanding what your system can hold without distortion. Concepts are included not as doctrine, but as orientation, so that what you experience first-hand can be recognized rather than dismissed.

A perceptual structure built only from second-hand explanation tends to remain fragile. It depends on memory and agreement. A structure built through lived experience becomes self-supporting. It stabilizes because it has been directly encountered.

This is why the explorations throughout the series are primary and the explanations are secondary. The aim is to allow your system to reorganize through engagement with your own experience.

The Material

What follows is not a set of instructions to master.

It is material to move through deliberately.

Each chapter builds upon the one before it. Within each chapter, sections unfold in a deliberate sequence. Later explorations rely on familiarity with earlier material. The progression is designed to support stability rather than intensity.

Although each book can be read independently, the five volumes together trace a gradual maturation of perception. Reading in sequence allows that development to unfold coherently. Insights, distinctions, and what you notice accumulate in an organized way, reinforcing rather than fragmenting one another.

This series assumes that lived experience cannot be rushed without becoming distorted. Depth requires pacing. Differentiation requires space. When experience is moved through too quickly, perception collapses into reaction or conclusion before it has fully organized.

For that reason, deliberate movement through the material matters. Not as discipline, but as protection of clarity.

This work is not oriented toward efficiency. It does not aim to streamline experience or make life move faster. Its purpose is different.

It creates the conditions under which meaning can form with greater accuracy and less distortion. That requires room. It requires pauses. It requires allowing your organismic intelligence to complete its own process before conclusion rushes in.

When life becomes optimized for speed alone, meaning tends to become thin. When the process is given space, meaning deepens.

This series is structured to protect that space.

You may begin wherever genuine curiosity arises, but depth comes from continuity.

Move at a pace you can integrate. A rhythm such as one chapter per week can support consolidation, but there is no advantage to speed. If something does not resolve immediately, allow it to remain open. Familiarity, not force, refines perception.

This is not a series to finish.

It is a series to live with.

Repetition and Familiarity

Repeating an exploration does not produce the same experience twice, and that is essential.

Perception refines through recurrence. Information that was once diffuse become distinguishable. Differentiation increases: sensation separates from emotion, emotion from narrative, internal experience from environmental input.

Clarity in this work does not arise from intensity or novelty. It develops through recognizing patterns as they appear across contexts.

Repetition stabilizes perception, while familiarity builds reliability.

Orientation, Not Instruction

The language in this series is meant to orient attention, not control it.

The explorations are not techniques to perform correctly. They are structured invitations to notice how perception is already functioning.

If something feels effortful or confusing, pause. Allow yourself to recalibrate rather than pushing for resolution. Strain narrows perception; steadiness widens it.

You are not training perception into something new.

You are allowing it to function with greater differentiation, stability, and trust.

Reading as Experience

As noted earlier, understanding in this series develops through first-hand experience.

No description here can define what you will notice. Each reader brings a different sensory history, emotional patterning, attentional habit, and environmental context. What becomes vivid for one person may be quiet for another.

There is no correct response to an exploration. The point is not to produce a particular sensation, insight, or state. It is to observe what is already present.

Some chapters may feel immediate and concrete. Others may seem abstract or uneventful. This does not indicate success or failure. Your organismic intelligence reorganizes in ways that are often subtle and individualized.

Trust your direct experience, even when it differs from expectation.

First-hand experience builds a world that explanation alone cannot.

— Adapted from Ingo Swann

SERIES INTRODUCTION

Consciousness

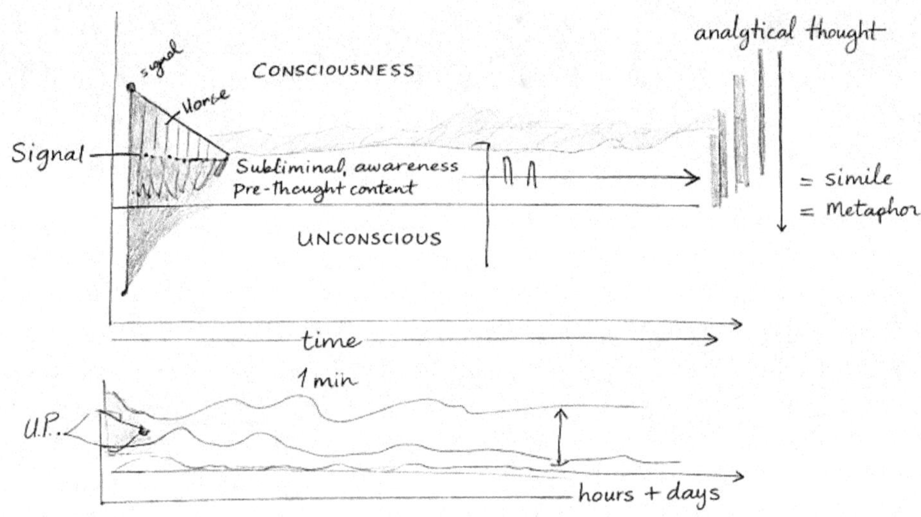

The Moment Before Thinking

Before you speak, act, or decide, something is already happening.

Sensation moves through the body. Emotional tone shifts. There is motion before thought.

These early signals often register as physiological changes: a slight tightening or softening in the chest or stomach, a change in breath, a lean forward or back, warmth in the hands, tension in the jaw.

They are understated and fast, often recognized only in hindsight.

This series begins there, before explanation, and before interpretation. It begins with direct experience of an interchange already unfolding between body, environment, and awareness.

> Something is received.
> Something becomes vivid.
> Something deepens.

These are not abstract concepts. They are ordinary biological processes already in motion.

The explorations in this series make that movement visible by creating the conditions for experience to register, rather than compelling attention.

A Language You Already Speak

You do not need to believe in anything new to begin.

> You already feel the atmosphere of a room the moment you walk in.
> You already notice when someone's attention is on you.
> You already sense when a conversation feels open, tense, guarded, or closed.

These capacities are not rare or reserved for a select few. They are human.

When your awareness is allowed to deepen, what you perceive does not arrive as a single cue. It has been differentiated: sensation separated into texture, tone, direction, temperature, affect, and meaning. Like light passing through a prism, your system reveals many qualities.

Attention determines which of those qualities come forward. Awareness receives them. Focus concentrates them.

This may sound abstract until you experience it directly. Differentiated information is not a theory. It is a lived sensory process.

The chapters ahead are designed to make that process accessible. Not by forcing attention, but by allowing it to reorganize from within. These are not techniques for producing experience, but orientations that let your perceptual awareness system reveal what is already occurring beneath habitual intellectual filters.

Attention vs. Awareness vs. Focus

To engage this movement, it is important to distinguish three interacting processes:

> Awareness is broad. It receives what is present.
> Attention is selective. It brings certain elements forward.
> Focus is narrow and sustained. It deepens engagement with what has been selected.

A simple way to remember:

> **Awareness** is the entire room.
> **Attention** is where you turn your head.
> **Focus** is what you examine closely.

Organismic intelligence does not collapse these into one function. It depends on their coordination. When they move coherently, your system clarifies before your intellect takes over.

How Perception Awakens Awareness

You may detect a shift in someone's voice, then discern the emotional tone behind it. You may feel the atmosphere of a room, then recognize whether it feels heavy, sharp, open, or calm.

This is organismic intelligence at work: perception registers; awareness receives; attention selects; focus intensifies.

The process becomes more comprehensible when you:

> allow your awareness to steady
> soften your attention rather than strain it
> remain with sensation long enough for meaning to surface
> track patterns rather than isolated data points
> stay grounded while noticing

When your attention is forced (narrowed by urgency or control) focus collapses into strain. Nuance disappears and everything begins to feel the same.

Modern culture continually pulls attention outward: noise, pressure, screens, speed. We stop noticing our own signals. We absorb moods that aren't ours. We sense that something is off but cannot locate why.

Like any instrument, organismic intelligence can drift out of tune. This series is about restoring that connection.

Why This Cannot Be Taught Like Information

Learning about the process and allowing your system itself to awaken follow very different rules.

Modern education excels at transmitting information: facts, systems, and procedures that can be standardized, measured, and repeated. Active awareness and organismic perception operate differently. They are not stabilized by external objects, not uniform across individuals, and not reliably shaped through repetition alone.

Organismic intelligence develops through calibration rather than accumulation, through attunement, feedback, and lived experience. It grows by becoming aware of how to detect, integrate, and respond to information in real time, not by memorization or procedural mastery.

As Ingo observed, information never enters a neutral mind. It arrives in an intellect already shaped by experience, emotion, culture, and expectation.

Each person perceives through an internal organization he referred to as a mind-map: habitual patterns of attention, interpretation, and association that influence what is allowed to register as meaningful or real. These patterns are not flaws. They are adaptive structures built through lived experience.

Layered onto this is what he called a reality box: the larger cultural framework that quietly defines which kinds of perceivable information is considered reasonable, trustworthy, or even possible. While mind-maps are personal, reality boxes are collective. Together, they shape what is noticed, what is dismissed, and what is never questioned.

Later books in this series explore these structures in greater depth: how they form, how they reinforce themselves, how they shape shared perception, and how they can become more flexible without destabilizing the system that depends on them.

Most of the time, these organizing patterns operate invisibly, influencing what is perceived long before we consciously reflect on them.

Because of this, your organismic intelligence cannot be installed by technique. It emerges when your attention steadies and reorganizes, and when your focus shifts from effort toward sustained presence.

Introductory Exploration A: Settling & Placing Attention

Objective

To let your attention gather naturally and place it without forcing.

Steps

1. Pause.
   - → Sit or stand comfortably. Let your body arrive where you are and allow your mind to follow.
   - → Notice that you are already aware: of the room, of your body, of this moment.
2. Steady.
   - → Feel the contact between your body and what supports you: floor, chair, ground.
   - → Allow your breath to move on its own. Do not regulate it. Simply notice its rhythm.
3. Gather your attention.
   - → Rather than directing it, allow your attention to collect in one neutral internal anchor.
   - → Choose one:
     - ÷ the natural rhythm of the breath
     - ÷ the weight of the body
     - ÷ a simple physical sensation (pressure, warmth, contact)
   - → Let your attention gather there the way water gathers in a basin: by gravity, not by force. If it drifts, notice the drift and gently return.
4. Rest.
   - → Allow your attention to remain with that anchor for 10–15 seconds.
   - → Nothing else needs to happen.

5. Focus your attention.
    → Now choose one simple object:
        ÷ a sound in the room
        ÷ a sensation in the body
        ÷ a neutral visual object
    → Direct your attention there softly.
    → Let the object come forward rather than reaching toward it.
    → Notice the difference between placing your attention and tightening
      around it (focusing on it).

Reflection

↺ Notice the difference between:
    → steadiness and effort
    → gathering your attention and forcing your focus
    → placing your attention and straining toward an object
↺ What changed when your attention was allowed to collect before being
   directed / focused?

Introductory Exploration B: The Prism Exercise

Objective

To experience differentiated attention directly.

Steps

1. Pause and focus on your breath.
2. Choose one neutral sensation in your body (pressure of clothing, weight,
   warmth).
3. Stay with it for 10–15 seconds.
4. Notice, without analysis:
    → texture (smooth, buzzing, dense, light)
    → temperature
    → movement (still, pulsing, drifting)
    → emotional tone (if any)
    → directional quality (inward, outward, downward)

Reflection

↺ Just note, this is not about creating new information, but about broadening the way you notice.

Introductory Exploration C: Forced vs. Receptive Attention

Objective

To feel the difference between effortful and receptive attention.

Steps

1. Look around the room and try to identify something important.
2. Notice tension in your eyes, breath, or attention.
3. Soften your gaze.
4. Let the room come to you without choosing.
5. Notice what registers first.

Reflection

↺ Which approach felt more evident?
↺ Which felt quieter?

How Awareness Actually Begins

The word *aware* comes from the Old English *gewær*, meaning watchful, vigilant, and attentive to what is happening around you.

It did not originally refer to inward thought, but to open receptivity, a readiness to be alert to shifts in the environment, in others, and within oneself.

Awareness, in this context, is receptive.

Attention highlights particular aspects of one's lived experience.

Focus deepens engagement with what has been highlighted.

Awareness awakens through simple shifts rather than effort. It begins when your attention slows enough for perception to take shape, not only within you, but between you and the world.

By the time your intellect explains it afterward, something is already unfolding within you and around you. You may recognize this when:

> a room feels tense or welcoming before anyone speaks
> a conversation shifts before the words change
> someone's presence is sensed before you see them
> your own state adjusts simply by entering a space
> you know someone is about to call just before the phone rings
> a person's smile appears friendly, yet something about it feels off
> you sense that an argument is forming before voices rise
> a place feels calm, unsettled, or heavy without an obvious reason
> you instinctively step aside just before someone passes behind you
> a situation feels promising (or troubling) before you can explain why

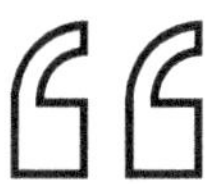

We ARE our sensing systems. And what we call "WE" or "US" or "SELF" is in some full part neither no more nor no less than our sensing systems are acknowledged, developed, and utilized.

— Adapted from Ingo Swann, *New Scientific Discoveries Regarding the Existence of Certain Psi Faculties*

This series dives into how to remain watchful without strain, receptive without overwhelm, and present without forcing perception.

About This Series

The five books are not primarily collections of theories.

They are structured explorations guided by orienting concepts.

Background ideas are introduced where necessary. They are not conclusions to adopt; instead, they are frameworks that help you navigate your own experience with greater clarity.

Each chapter offers opportunities for direct experience. These are practical ways to observe and work with your own organismic intelligence as it unfolds in real time.

This is not about adopting a belief system.

It is about learning to notice what moves within you and what circulates around you.

Throughout the series you will practice grounding, centering, attunement, and stabilization.

These capacities form the basis of organismic intelligence: the intrinsic regulatory and perceptual intelligence of a living system in continuous exchange with its environment.

No prior training or specialized background is required.

Only curiosity... and a willingness to observe your own experience with care and precision.

GETTING READY

Before beginning the explorations, it helps to approach them in a way that supports regulation and continuity within ordinary life.

This section provides orientation rather than warning. Depth here develops through stability, not intensity.

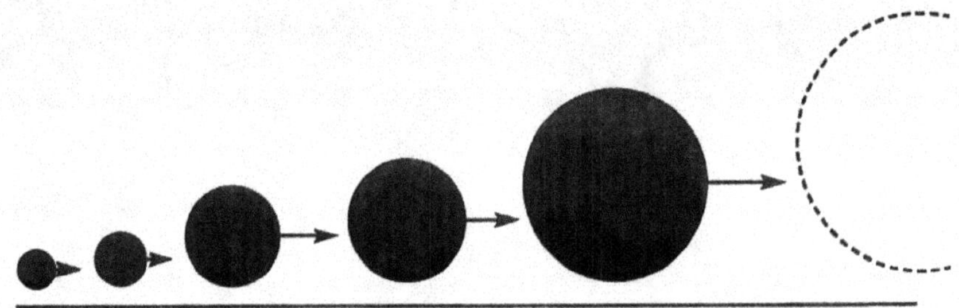

DEVELOPMENT

About Clarity, Not Identity

This series is not about becoming special, advanced, or exceptional. Perceptual clarity tends to reduce certainty rather than inflate it.

It softens reactivity and sharpens discernment.

If what you perceive begins to feel separating, elevating, or identity-forming, return to grounding and simplicity.

Trust stability more than intensity.

Organismic perception and active awareness are usually neutral.

Drama is not a sign of accuracy.

Go Slowly

Perceptual development does not reward speed. Reading quickly, stacking practices, or chasing insight tends to produce confusion rather than clarity.

Some sections may land unnoticed and deepen later. Some practices may feel elusive rather than dramatic. Some understanding may arrive days or weeks after reading. That is not delay. It is integration.

Let this discovery move at the pace your system can genuinely hold.

Pause If You Need To

If you experience emotional destabilization, persistent anxiety, difficulty staying oriented in daily life, intrusive imagery, or loss of grounding, pause your engagement with the material.

Return to ordinary routines. Move your body. Rest. Seek support if needed.

Pausing is not failure. It is perceptual maturity.

Boxed Spaces

Throughout the five books, you will notice spaces set aside for notes and observations for what you are noticing.

These are not assignments to complete or conclusions to reach. They are holding spaces where your system can notice what is forming as it reorganizes.

Not everything arrives as conscious reasoning.

Some information appears as sensation, spatial sense, image, movement, or an unformed impression that does not yet have words.

Writing things down helps stabilize these early clues without forcing them into interpretation.

You are encouraged to use these spaces in whatever way feels natural. A few words, a phrase, a line, or even a single mark are often enough.

The purpose is not to explain what you experienced, but simply to acknowledge that something registered.

In addition to written notes, you may find it helpful to sketch, diagram, or draw as part of the process. These drawings are not meant to be illustrative or artistic.

They are another way your system organizes itself.

As Ingo observed, perceptual processing systems often work ahead of conscious reasoning.

When this happens, drawing can become a direct extension of the process instead of a representation of it.

The hand may move without deliberate planning, and the image may take shape without apparent decision-making or conscious intent.

In such moments, the drawing is not merely a sketch of conscious impressions; it is part of the perceptual process itself.

You may notice that shapes, lines, or spatial relationships appear before you understand what they refer to.

For now, the focus is on simply noticing these impressions as they arise. The question of how meaning forms from them is taken up in Book Three.

Keeping a simple journal alongside this book can support this process. It does not need to be detailed or analytical. A notebook, loose pages, or a digital document will work.

The purpose is not to track progress, but to give information a place to land while it is still organizing itself.

Write or draw only what feels appropriate in the moment. If nothing comes, that is also information. Perceptual clarity develops through continuity, not pressure.

These practices are not about capturing experience correctly. They are about making room for your system to complete its own work.

Approaching the Explorations

This series does not ask you to adopt or defend a belief system.

Nothing here depends on agreement with metaphysical claims or commitment to a particular worldview.

You are asked only to notice your own experience and begin to discern how perception functions.

Perception does not become accurate because it feels meaningful, and meaning does not become reliable because it feels vivid.

The material herein emphasizes recognition over assumption and discernment over interpretation.

The explorations that follow are temporary orientations. They are designed to help you notice specific dynamics, not to create permanent states. When an exploration concludes, allow your system to return to its natural baseline.

If something does not resonate, there is no need to force it. Familiarity develops through repetition and steadiness, not intensity.

What matters is not what you perceive, but how your perceptual awareness system (your organismic intelligence) begins to organize itself as your attention steadies.

About the "What to Watch For" and "Reflection" Sections

Each exploration includes a brief *What to Watch* For list. These are not predictions or guarantees.

They are orientation points: examples of common responses meant to help you recognize shifts rather than overlook them.

If your experience differs from what is listed, that is simply your organismic intelligence (your perceptual awareness system) responding through its own patterns.

The list exists to expand possibility, not constrain it.

Each section also includes reflection prompts designed to support noticing and help you articulate what is already present in your experience.

These are not questions to answer correctly, but invitations to engage more directly. If other questions arise, you are encouraged to follow them as well.

Keeping a simple record of sensations, impressions, or recurring shifts can help patterns become visible over time without forcing interpretation.

The purpose is recognition, not analysis.

Staying Close to Sensation

At times, noticing may include images, impressions, or fleeting associations.

There is no need to interpret these immediately.

Early data often communicates through sensation and tone before meaning becomes lucid. If something feels vivid, unusual, or emotionally charged, simply return to grounding and stay with what is directly felt.

Meaning clarifies through familiarity, repetition, and context, not urgency.

When you remain close to sensation, clarity tends to emerge on its own.

Ground first. Always

If at any point the material feels overwhelming, inflated, destabilizing, or "too open," return immediately to what is most basic: breath, posture, physical sensation, and ordinary orientation.

Clarity begins in the body. Organismic perception does not replace grounding; it depends on it.

Grounding prevents drift into imagination. Centering prevents sensitivity from becoming overwhelming.

Together they form the foundation for everything that follows.

A One-Minute Practice

1. Pause.
2. Feel a connection with the floor or chair.
3. Let your breath slow naturally.
4. Stay with one sensation in your body. This is where awareness begins.

Simple reset practices for reestablishing grounding and orientation are included in the Appendix and may be returned to at any time.

Working with Your Eyes

Soft eyes support relational awareness. Closed eyes support internal sensing. You will explore both throughout this series. How you use your eyes influences how your attention organizes itself.

When vision is held tightly, attention narrows and shifts toward analysis. When the eyes soften or close, attention redistributes, allowing other perceptual signals to become more available. The following exploration introduces this shift.

Introductory Exploration D: Soft Eyes vs. Closed Eyes

Objective

To explore how eye tension and relaxation influence attention and perception.

Setup

Sit comfortably in a neutral environment. No special posture required.

Steps

1. Phase 1: Normal Vision
   - → Look around the room normally.
   - → Notice how your eyes focus and select.
2. Phase 2: Soft Eyes
   - → Without closing your eyes, loosen the muscles around them.
   - → Allow your vision to become less sharp, more panoramic.
   - → Notice what changes without trying to make anything happen.
3. Phase 3: Closed Eyes
   - → Close your eyes.
   - → Shift your focus to non-visual sensing (breath, posture, pressure, tone).

What to Watch For

With normal vision:

- ⟩ attention narrows
- ⟩ thought increases
- ⟩ posture tightens

With soft eyes:

> attention diffuses
> surroundings feel more spacious
> body tension decreases

With closed eyes:

> internal awareness becomes more distinct
> understated texture or tone becomes more noticeable
> distraction decreases

Why This Happens

Softening or closing your eyes:

> reduces your visual dominance (a major "information jammer")
> allows your attention to widen
> shifts your focus from analysis to noticing
> decreases your sympathetic nervous system activation
> enhances your interoception (your sense of internal bodily signals such as breathing, tension, or calm) and your spatial awareness

When vision relaxes, other perceptual channels become available.

Reflection

↺ Which of the three states felt most relaxed?
↺ Which allowed you to notice more subtle cues?
↺ How did your body respond in each phase?

Key Takeaway

You are not shutting out the world.

You are shifting how you receive it.

Begin Where You Are

You are already wired for perception. You are already an instrument.

This book simply creates the conditions for you to listen.

What follows is not something to get right.

It is an invitation to notice what is already happening.

There is always more occurring in perception than what reaches conscious awareness. Subtle signals move alongside ordinary seeing and hearing, registering before thought intervenes.

When we restrict ourselves only to what appears immediately measurable, perception contracts and experience becomes rigid.

But when awareness is allowed to widen, perception moves freely beyond familiar boundaries.

— Adapted from Ingo Swann, *Cosmic Art*

NOTICING

WHAT'S ALREADY THERE

This book does not begin by expanding perception. It begins by clarifying it.

Before what you perceive becomes refined, it must become stable.

Before it becomes expansive, it must become trustworthy.

Book One is about restoring contact with the perceptual processes that quietly organize everyday experience.

You will notice how sensation precedes thought, how attention shifts before decisions are made, and how atmosphere communicates before words are spoken.

These are lived events not abstract ideas.

This is not about heightening sensitivity. It is about differentiating what is already occurring.

But more importantly, it is about noticing:

> how your body registers shifts in tone and presence
> how space itself influences perception
> how your attention organizes meaning without commentary
> how ease and pressure signal different relational states

These are not special abilities. They are structural features of organismic perception that often operate without recognition.

Book One provides experiences through which these processes gradually come into view, approached through steadiness rather than intensity.

By the end, perception may feel simpler, not more dramatic, more grounded, not more amplified, less mysterious, more direct.

Nothing is being added here. Your instrument is simply being tuned.

1 | What Happens Between
Presence, Attention, & Atmosphere

Opening Invitation

Begin by simply noticing what is already unfolding around you:

> People subtly adjust when attention reaches them.
> Rooms carry a discernible emotional tone.
> Groups fall into rhythm without speaking.
> A presence often felt before footsteps or sound.

These are not private impressions or interpretive guesses.

They are:

> relational signals
> patterns of interaction that your system both generates and registers as part of ordinary social and environmental awareness

This chapter begins with what can be observed externally.

Rather than turning inward, you are invited to notice:

> how attention, presence, and atmosphere behave in everyday situations
> how information between people and environments organizes itself, often without conscious coordination

No analysis, interpretation, or assumption is required.

The focus is on:

> watching what happens when attention shifts
> when people enter or leave a space
> when tone changes without words

These observations provide a shared reference point.

They establish that what is happening does not begin inside the individual alone but emerges within a relational space that is already active and responsive.

Relational Tone

Your Personal Presence

Every person carries a recognizable presence shaped by:

> breath
> posture
> muscular tension
> emotional tone
> attention
> nervous system rhythm

These qualities are not hidden. They are continuously expressed.

When your internal rhythm shifts, others often respond (sometimes subtly, sometimes immediately) through changes in attention, posture, or tone.

This offers your first direct evidence that perception is relational. You are constantly interacting with the environment around you, and you can observe this interaction clearly.

Group Atmosphere

Emotion moves through groups like weather:

> tone spreads
> breath synchronizes
> nervous systems attune
> posture and pacing align

This is biology interacting with perception.

Human nervous systems are responsive and social by design.

What we call atmosphere is the felt result of this coordination.

You are not separate from it.

You continuously participate in it through your own state.

Notes.

EXPLORATION 1.1: The Attention Effect

Attuning to One Another

Objective

To observe how human attention can be detectable to another person.

Setup

Go to a public place such as a café, park, airport, or waiting area. Choose someone neutral and appropriate to observe, keeping your demeanor relaxed and respectful.

Steps

1. Sit or stand naturally.
2. Choose a person who is not currently aware of you.
3. Let your attention rest gently in their general direction (toward the back of the body or presence in space).
4. Do not stare or concentrate. Keep your attention light and non-intrusive.
5. Notice what happens.
6. Observe how long it takes before the person subtly shifts posture, orientation, or awareness of you.

What to Watch For

> a small head tilt or posture shift
> a brief pause in activity
> a scan of the environment
> a sensation in your own body (warmth, tingling, pressure), your internal sensations may reflect a moment of connection rather than cause it

Reflection

↺ About how long did it take?
↺ What did you notice in your own body?
↺ Did the moment have a distinct texture?

Why This Happens

Humans have an extended sensory zone known as peripersonal space. It is the lived region of active awareness surrounding the body.

When attention enters that space:

> nervous systems orient
> movement patterns adjust
> perceptual awareness systems registers change
> emotional tone recalibrates

Attention is not just a thought. It behaves like a nuanced form of interaction.

Notes.

EXPLORATION 1.2: The Mood Weather
Emotional Atmosphere in Groups

Objective

To notice how groups generate atmosphere beyond verbal exchange.

Setup

Observe a small group in a natural setting (café, workplace, park, waiting area).

Steps

1. Take a moment to sit or stand quietly without focusing on any one person. Allow your attention to rest in the space as a whole.
2. Look with a soft, unfocused gaze.
3. Describe the atmosphere internally, without judgment, using simple qualities such as:
    → light
    → heavy
    → tense
    → playful
    → flat
4. Notice how your own body responds.
5. Observe what shifts when someone enters or leaves.

What to Watch For

⟩ a sudden lift or drop in mood
⟩ one person changing the group's tone
⟩ synchronization of posture or rhythm
⟩ immediate bodily responses in you (your body often responds to group dynamics before your thoughts catch up)

Reflection

↺ How did the group's atmosphere affect you?
↺ What shifted when the group changed?

Why This Happens

Humans are biologically organized for social attunement. Group environments function as shared regulatory systems rather than isolated individuals occupying the same space.

When people gather:

> attention synchronizes
> posture and rhythm begin to align
> breathing patterns shift in response to one another
> emotional tone distributes across the group
> nervous systems recalibrate in relation to proximity and movement

What we experience as atmosphere is the accumulated effect of these small adjustments.

Notes.

EXPLORATION 1.3: Observation & Interpretation
When Meaning Is Added to What You Notice

Objective

To distinguish between what you directly observe and what you automatically conclude. The deeper structure of how meaning forms will be explored in Books Three and Five. For now, noticing the distinction is enough.

Setup

Observe a neutral interaction in a public setting (a café, workplace, park, waiting area), or recall a recent interaction that felt noticeable but not dramatic.

Choose something ordinary. This is not about analyzing intense situations. It is about noticing in everyday contexts.

Steps

1. Select a person or small interaction to observe quietly and respectfully.
2. Internally describe only what is directly observable:
   → posture
   → distance between people
   → pace of movement
   → rhythm or volume of speech
   → facial expression
   → direction of gaze
3. Pause.
4. Notice what conclusions arise automatically:
   → They seem irritated.
   → They look distracted.
   → They are in agreement.
   → Something feels tense.
5. Separate the two:
   → What did you directly observe?
   → What did you add in order to make *sense* of it?
6. Return to simple observation for a few moments without correcting or suppressing interpretation. Just notice the difference.

What to Watch For

> how quickly explanation forms
> how convincing conclusions feel
> shifts in your body when simply observing versus interpreting
> changes in emotional tone when the story softens

Reflection

↺ What remained when you removed explanation?
↺ Where in your body did conclusions feel strongest?

Why This Happens

Perception and interpretation are distinct but closely linked processes. When you observe an interaction:

> sensory details are registered
> emotional tone is detected
> prior experience activates
> expectations influence meaning
> conclusions form rapidly and often unconsciously

These processes are natural. They allow fast social navigation. Difficulty arises only when direct observation and added interpretation merge without you being aware.

Notes.

EXPLORATION 1.4: The Ripple Effect
The Effect of Presence on Space

Objective

To notice how changes in your internal state are registered in the surrounding environment (often before words, intention, or conscious interaction are involved). This exploration is not about influencing others. It is about recognizing how presence is already felt and responded to.

Setup

Choose a familiar environment where your presence would be natural and unobtrusive: a workplace, a shared living space, a café you regularly visit, or a waiting area. The setting should feel ordinary. Avoid situations where people are engaged in intense or private conversations. You are not attempting to create a reaction. You are observing how your internal state and external space interact.

Steps

1. Enter a room naturally, without adjusting your pace, posture, or attention.
2. Observe how people and the space feel as you enter.
3. Leave the room.
4. Allow a brief interval (a few minutes is sufficient) for the environment to recalibrate.
5. Re-enter with slower breath, relaxed posture, and a softer, more grounded pace.
6. Notice what registers, without trying to create or interpret an effect.

What to Watch For

⟩ people looking up or pausing without an obvious reason
⟩ slight shifts in conversational flow or rhythm
⟩ changes in your own internal sense of ease, density, or coherence
⟩ the room feeling momentarily more alert, quieter, or more open

Reflection

↺ What changed when you changed?
↺ What seemed to register before anyone spoke or reacted?

Integration Practice 1
What Did You Notice?

Spend 3–5 minutes reflecting:

- ↺ Which exploration surprised you?
- ↺ Which internal state was the strongest?
- ↺ Did any moment feel unmistakably real?
- ↺ What did you notice about your attention?

This is not analysis. It is a gentle acknowledgment.

Observations.

Closing Thought

This chapter reopens a door you have already walked through many times.

> Your body is organized to respond to relationship, proximity, and change.
> Your awareness is not confined to your skin but responds to what is around you.
> Your attention participates in the world in observable ways.

No new capacity has been created.

What was already happening has simply come into focus.

2 | Your Body, the Antenna
The In-Body Experience

Opening Invitation

In the previous chapter, you observed how your attention meets what surrounds you.

Now the focus shifts inward, to the instrument through which that meeting is registered.

Perception requires a system capable of responding to change.

That system is not abstract awareness or thought. It is the body itself.

Your body registers information before it explains it. It continually adjusts to pressure, temperature, movement, tension, expansion, contraction, and shifts in emotional tone. These adjustments occur prior to interpretation and often before conscious meaning is assigned.

In everyday life, much of this internal sensing remains in the backgrounded or overlooked.

This chapter brings it forward, not to analyze it, but so that you can become familiar with how information arrives through sensation.

The emphasis here is simple internal noticing:

⟩ becoming aware of physical sensation from within
⟩ allowing your breath to regulate naturally
⟩ restoring awareness of sensory channels that may have been silenced through habit or distraction

This is not an exercise in watching thoughts or producing insight. It is an invitation to notice how information feels when perception is grounded in the body rather than filtered through speculation.

In Chapter 1, you observed how perception unfolds in the space between people and environments.

In Chapter 2, you begin calibrating the instrument that makes such perception possible.

As your internal awareness becomes clearer, the process stabilizes. What follows in later chapters depends on this grounding, not as a technique, but as a condition for reliable awareness.

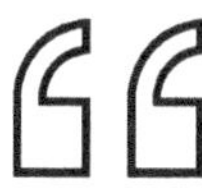

Reality is structured. Long before it is analyzed, it is encountered. By participating in it, you come to recognize its patterns.

— Adapted from Ingo Swann, *Contaminants and "Noise"*

Notes.

EXPLORATION 2.1: The Body Scan Reset
Reconnecting with Internal Sensation

Objective

To reestablish contact with internal sensation. This is the baseline of organismic perception.

Setup

Sit comfortably, feet grounded. No special posture required.

Steps

1. Close your eyes briefly.
2. Focus on your feet.
3. Simply notice (warm, cool, buzzing, neutral, numb).
4. Widen your focus, letting your attention move slowly upward through your legs.
5. Notice your belly, chest, and shoulders.
6. Continue moving your attention into your arms, hands, neck, and head.
7. Do not change anything you find. Just notice.

What to Watch For

⟩ temperature differences
⟩ tingling or buzzing
⟩ heaviness or lightness
⟩ quiet or muted areas
⟩ emotion expressed physically before thought

Reflection

↻ Which areas felt most present?
↻ Which felt distant or quiet?
↻ Did any of those quieter areas feel neutral, unfamiliar, or protective?

Why This Happens

The body scan brings your internal awareness forward by directing your attention through your body in a slow, systematic way.

In everyday activity, your attention tends to move outward toward tasks, conversations, and external events. As a result, much of what is occurring within your body remains unnoticed. Sensation is still present, but it often stays in the background of your awareness.

Moving your attention gradually through your body allows these internal experiences to come into view. Areas that feel vivid, muted, neutral, or distant can reveal how what you are aware of has been distributed across your body.

Notes.

EXPLORATION 2.2: Breath as a Regulator
Stabilizing Organismic Perception

Objective

To reduce your internal interference so your organismic perception can organize itself with greater clarity and stability.

Setup

Sit or stand comfortably with relaxed shoulders. Allow your spine to be upright but not rigid. Let your hands rest naturally. There is no need for a special posture.

Steps

1. Take a moment to notice your current internal state.
2. Inhale slowly through the nose for 4 seconds.
3. Hold your breath gently for 2 seconds without strain.
4. Exhale slowly through your mouth or nose for 6 seconds.
5. Allow the exhale to soften the body naturally.
6. Repeat this cycle for 6 rounds.

What to Watch For

> warmth spreading through your torso or hands
> tension loosening or melting in your shoulders, jaw, or belly
> your breath becoming smoother
> sounds and bodily sensations becoming easier to notice
> your attention relaxing into the present moment
> a calm, alert state rather than heaviness or drowsiness

Reflection

↻ How did your internal state shift before and after the breath cycle?
↻ Did your attention feel more settled or more dispersed?
↻ Did your bodily sensation become clearer, softer, or more continuous?

Why This Happens: Interoception

As noted earlier, you have a built-in perceptual sense called interoception. It is the body's capacity to perceive its own internal activity: heartbeat, breath, pressure, temperature, and overall physiological state.

Organismic perception depends on the clarity of this internal awareness. What you perceive is always a combination of outer input and inner sensation. When internal information is faint or overridden by stress, your attention becomes dominated by external stimuli. When it is available and steady, information becomes more integrated and precise.

Breath plays a direct role in this process. A longer, slower exhale supports nervous system regulation, allowing your body to shift out of stress-driven activation. As regulation increases, internal interference decreases and interoceptive activity becomes easier to notice.

Notes.

EXPLORATION 2.3: The Hand Proximity Effect

Pressure & Sensation Near the Body

Objective

To notice how your body registers pressure, distance, and relation in near-body space.

Setup

Stand or sit with your arms relaxed.

Steps

1. Rub your palms together for about 5 seconds.
2. Separate your hands to roughly a foot apart.
3. Slowly bring them closer, pausing when sensation changes.
4. Gently compress and expand the space between your hands.
5. Let your attention steady on the space and notice what registers in your awareness.

What to Watch For

> pressure or resistance
> warmth
> tingling or pulsing
> a subtle push or pull
> a sense of density or thickness

Reflection

↺ How did the space between your hands register through sensation?
↺ What words or images best describe what you noticed?
↺ Did the sensation change as your attention steadied?
↺ How did the sensation vary from moment to moment?
↺ Did it feel faint, uneven, steady, or changeable?

What You're Noticing

What you notice arises from several overlapping processes:

> bioelectric activity
> thermal awareness
> steady attention
> spatial mapping near your body
> boundary perception (where you and space meet; introduced here, expanded later in the series)
> proprioceptive adjustments (your body's internal sense of position, movement, and muscle tension)

Together, these processes create perceptual coherence. For many people, this is when perception shifts from concept to embodied experience.

Notes.

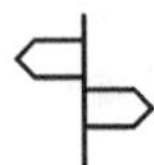

So, What Is "Perceptual Coherence"?

In this series, perceptual coherence refers to the integrated condition that arises when the body is sensing, regulating, and orienting in relation to its environment.

It includes:

> bodily sensation
> spatial awareness near the skin
> bioelectric and thermal activity
> attentional presence
> the body's capacity to detect proximity, pressure, and relation

Perceptual coherence is not something you imagine or project. It is not an added layer or special state. It reflects how your body is already organizing information in real time.

When you notice warmth, resistance, tingling, density, or a defined edge near your hands or body, you are not detecting an abstract concept.

You are registering the functional activity of a living organism interacting with space.

This does not replace the body or extend it beyond itself. It describes how bodily sensing becomes relational: how your system attunes to contact, distance, and influence without requiring interpretation.

In this book, coherence is introduced as an observable condition. In Book Two, we examine its architecture more deeply: how it stabilizes, how it becomes disrupted, how it is restored, and how it shapes boundaries, emotion, and relational exchange.

What matters here is direct observation.

INTEGRATION PRACTICE 2
A Simple Daily Sequence

For the next 24 hours, repeat this sequence once or twice:

1. **Body Scan** (30 seconds): note 3 internal sensations.
2. **Breath Cycle** (1 minute): inhale 4 → hold 2 → exhale 6.
3. **Hand Space** (30 seconds): notice the space between your palms.

This sequence is meant to stabilize your system, not intensify sensation, so what you register becomes clearer and more consistent over time. If sensation feels faint or ordinary, that is appropriate. Stability precedes clarity.

Observations.

Closing Thought

Before you can notice the world clearly, you must feel yourself.

> Your body senses.
> Your awareness notices change.
> Your breath regulates coherence.

When these align, your perceptual awareness system becomes grounded and organismic, able to register what is present without strain or projection.

In the next chapter, attention moves outward again, into the space between things.

3 | The Space Between
Where Perception Becomes Physical

Opening Invitation

What you perceive does not exist only inside you. Nor is it separate from you. Organismic perception emerges through interaction, at the boundary where your body meets the world.

You have already encountered this:

> the pressure shift when someone stands too close
> the pull or ease you feel around certain people
> the tightness that lingers after conflict
> the warm or cool tone of a room
> the boundary your body responds to without conscious explanation

These are not ideas or interpretations.

They are relational sensations that describe how your body responds to proximity, tone, and influence in its immediate environment.

This chapter focuses on noticing relational texture directly. Not through imagination or visualization, but through the body's response to space, distance, and contact.

Here, perception becomes tangible.

Not conceptual.

Not symbolic.

Physical.

EXPLORATION 3.1: The Air Pressure Effect

Pressure & Distance Near the Body

Objective

To notice the pressure and texture just outside your skin: the first threshold of gathering information beyond direct touch.

Setup

Sit or stand comfortably with one hand extended.

Steps

1. Extend one palm outward.
2. With the other hand, slowly move your palm toward it, as if approaching water.
3. Keep your attention on the space between your hands, not on your hands themselves.
4. Pause when you notice resistance, warmth, density, or gentle pushback.
5. Stay with the sensation briefly and let it stabilize.

What to Watch For

> a cushiony or balloon-like feeling
> a sense of thicker or "charged" air
> subtle warmth or temperature gradients
> a faint magnetic push or soft boundary

Reflection

↺ What word best describes what you felt? (Choose words that feels accurate rather than impressive.)
↺ Did the sensation appear suddenly or gradually?
↺ Did it feel steady, faint, or changeable?
↺ Did the distance between your hands affect what you noticed?
↺ Did the sensation feel more like pressure, temperature, texture, or something else?

Why This Happens

Several processes overlap here:

> spatial mapping: your nervous system tracks space around your body
> thermal gradients: warmth radiates from living tissue
> bioelectric activity: living systems generate measurable signals
> steady attention: sensitivity increases when your system stabilizes

You are not imagining pressure. You are registering proximity.

<table>
<tr><td>

Notes.

</td></tr>
</table>

EXPLORATION 3.2: Near-Body Coherence

Experiencing Form & Structure

Objective

To notice how sensation near your body organizes itself into form, boundary, and responsiveness.

Setup

Rub your hands together for 5 seconds.

Steps

1. Hold your hands roughly a foot apart, palms facing.
2. Slowly move them toward each other.
3. Pause when the sensation changes or becomes more defined.
4. Gently compress and expand the space between your hands.
5. Rotate your hands and notice how the sensation shifts with orientation.

What to Watch For

> elastic resistance
> increasing warmth
> tingling or pulsing
> a sense of fullness or containment
> a subtle push or pull

Reflection

↺ How did the sensation organize itself as your hands moved?
↺ Did it feel soft, firm, light, dense, or variable?
↺ What changed when you paused or altered orientation?

Why This Matters

This exploration highlights how you can discern structure in space without relying on visualization or imagination.

For many people, this is a moment when perception becomes unmistakably physical. Not dramatic, but tangible. Attention steadies, sensation gains definition, and space no longer feels empty, but responsive.

No new capacity is being generated.

What is already occurring becomes easier to recognize.

This is organismic intelligence in direct experience.

Notes.

EXPLORATION 3.3: Material Presence
Sensing Materials Without Touch

Objective

To notice how different materials register through sensation and proximity, without relying on touch or interpretation.

Setup

Gather three items:

1. Something living (plant, fruit, leaf).
2. Something metallic.
3. Something natural (wood, stone, fabric).

Steps

1. Move your hand slowly a few inches above and around the living object.
2. Notice texture, warmth, or movement.
3. Repeat with the metallic object.
4. Repeat with wood, stone, or fabric.

What to Watch For

> warmth, coolness, or neutrality
> density versus openness
> buzzing versus stillness
> subtle tonal differences

Reflection

↺ How did different materials register through sensation?
↺ Did any feel active, warm, sharp, neutral, diffuse, or grounded?
↺ Which object registered most well-defined?
↺ Which surprised you?

Why Objects Register Differently

Different materials interact with you in different ways:

> living systems generate ongoing bioelectric activity
> metals alter electromagnetic conditions
> natural materials retain heat and structural resonance uniquely

You are noticing distinct sensory qualities that arise from how different forms organize energy, temperature, and structure in space.

Notes.

INTEGRATION PRACTICE 3
The 10-Second Space Check

In daily life, organismic perception is usually already available. This integration practice briefly and gently returns your attention to it.

Several times a day:

1. Bring your attention to the air in front of your body. Is it neutral, thick, warm, or cool?
2. Briefly bring your hands together and notice the boundary.
3. Observe how your body responds to proximity (leaning in, easing back, softening, or tensing).

These brief moments can reawaken spatial awareness, a capacity modern life often dulls.

Observations.

Closing Thought

In the physical world, things meet through direct contact.

In organismic perception, they meet through relation; through proximity, pressure, texture, and response.

This becomes undeniable when you begin to notice:

> the density or openness of the air
> the felt boundary of your skin
> the texture and resistance of objects
> the space that forms between people

You are not acquiring a new sense.

You are recognizing an underlying organization you have been living within all along.

Insight rarely arrives through proclamation or dramatic realization.

It often comes sideways, through familiarity, repetition, and recognition, when something that was once background becomes obvious.

In the next chapter, what you notice widens to include the character of rooms and environments, and how space itself shapes perception through tone, structure, and atmosphere.

4 | The Living Room
The Atmosphere of Places

Earlier chapters emphasized detection. Here, the emphasis shifts to how your attention meets what is already present.

Opening Invitation

Rooms have weather:

> Some feel bright and breathable.
> Some feel stagnant the moment you step inside.
> Some relax your system.
> Others tighten it for no obvious reason.

You are not imagining this.

Your body is already responding to architecture, airflow, sound, light, angles, and the emotional imprint of activity long before your intellect engages.

This chapter is not about people. It is about place:

> how rooms hold memory
> how atmosphere forms
> how environments shape mood, clarity, and perceptual experience

Spaces communicate.

Your body is already reading them.

EXPLORATION 4.1: Room Temperature Without Temperature

The Emotional Tone of a Space

Objective

To notice the atmospheric quality of a room without relying on visual cues or analysis.

Setup

Choose two rooms with contrasting activity levels: a quieter space (bedroom, closet) and a more active space (kitchen, living room, workspace).

Steps

1. Stand in the doorway of the first room.
2. Soften your eyes or close them briefly.
3. Step inside slowly, as if entering water.
4. Bring your attention to the atmosphere using simple qualities:
    → warm
    → cool
    → neutral
    → heavy
    → bright
    → quiet
5. Move to the second room and repeat.
6. Compare what you notice.

What to Watch For

> changes in your breathing
> shifts in your posture
> expansion or contraction in your chest or belly
> buzzing, stillness, or density
> a felt "emotional temperature"

Reflection

↺ Which room felt most alive?
↺ Which felt dense or stagnant?
↺ What words came naturally as you tried to describe those differences?

Why Rooms Hold Emotion

Spaces register human activity. Every emotional moment produces:

> sound
> muscular tension
> breath patterns
> movement
> shifts in nervous system activity

Walls, floors, and objects absorb these patterns over time, creating residual atmosphere. This is not hauntings or symbolism, but the lingering imprint of lived experience.

Children notice it. Animals notice it. Your body notices it.

Notes.

EXPLORATION 4.2: The Threshold Effect
The Contrast Between Spaces

Objective

To notice how atmosphere shifts when moving from one space to another.

Setup

Choose two connected spaces, such as:

1. hallway → bedroom
2. kitchen → living room
3. indoors → outdoors
4. car → house

Steps

1. Stand with one foot in each space.
2. Pause and notice the contrast.
3. Step fully into one room.
4. Notice changes in:
     → posture
     → mood
     → breath
     → openness
5. Step back into the other space.

What to Watch For

〉 immediate emotional shifts
〉 pressure or lightness
〉 relief or contraction
〉 non-thermal temperature changes

Reflection

↻ Which space felt supportive?
↻ Which felt draining or tense?
↻ What did you notice about when your body recorded the shift?

Why Rooms Feel Different

Rooms tend to feel distinct because multiple sensory variables shift at once:

> light intensity and spectrum change (how bright the light is and the range of colors it contains)
> acoustic properties vary (echo, reverberation, and sound dampening)
> spatial proportion shifts (ceiling height, enclosure, or openness, which affect how the room visually scales)
> surface texture and flooring modify somatosensory input (information gathered through touch, pressure, and contact with surfaces)
> airflow, temperature, and scent subtly differ
> memories and learned associations may be contextually triggered

These inputs are processed simultaneously across several perceptual systems:

> visual (what you see)
> auditory (what you hear)
> somatosensory (touch, pressure, and body contact with surfaces)
> vestibular (your sense of balance, orientation, and movement in space)
> interoceptive (your awareness of internal bodily states such as breath, tension, and temperature)

In this way, a room is not merely a container of objects. It is a dynamic configuration of sensory conditions that continuously modulates perception, physiology, and behavioral readiness.

Notes.

EXPLORATION 4.3: The Corner Effect
Variation Within a Single Room

Objective

To detect variations in atmosphere within one space.

Setup

Choose any room with four corners.

Steps

1. Stand in the first corner for 10–20 seconds.
2. Notice heaviness, neutrality, or liveliness.
3. Move to the next corner and repeat.
4. Continue around the room.

What to Watch For

> dense or stagnant corners
> charged or active corners
> calm or neutral zones.
> noticeable contrasts between locations

Reflection

↺ Which corner felt most supportive or settling?
↺ Which felt uncomfortable or constricting?
↺ What did you notice about how your body responded in each location?

Why Corners Matter

Corners tend to feel distinct because several factors converge there:

> sound reflects and lingers
> airflow slows or changes direction
> movement and activity naturally concentrate
> your awareness heightens at boundaries and transitions

Together, these conditions make corners more perceptually distinct. They are places where slight variations become more noticeable, not because something is stored there, but because organismic perception sharpens at edges.

Animals often gravitate toward particular areas in a room for this reason. This exploration invites you to notice how spatial structures influence you, quietly, without interpretation.

Notes.

EXPLORATION 4.4: The Room Reset
Presence & the Atmosphere of Space

Objective

To observe how your internal state interacts with a space.

Setup

Choose a familiar room. Walk through the room once at a normal pace and briefly notice how the space feels.

Steps

1. Stand or sit near the center of the room.
2. Allow your shoulders, jaw, and belly to soften.
3. Slow your breathing slightly, letting the exhale lengthen naturally.
4. Remain still for 20–30 seconds, allowing your attention to encompass the room as a whole.
5. Without forcing any particular feeling, simply remain present.
6. After this pause, walk through the room again and notice whether anything about the atmosphere feels different.

What to Watch For

> a calmer overall tone in the room
> reduced heaviness in certain areas
> lighter or clearer air
> greater internal steadiness as you move
> shifts in how welcoming, neutral, or settled the room feels

Reflection

↺ Did you notice any shift in how the room felt before and after the pause?
↺ Did your own internal state change as your breathing slowed?
↺ Did the space feel different as you moved through it the second time?
↺ Did certain areas of the room feel more comfortable or neutral?

Why This Happens

The atmosphere of a room is shaped by many sensory conditions (light, sound, spatial proportions, temperature, and airflow). These features remain relatively constant, but how they are perceived depends partly on the state of the body registering them.

When your breathing slows and muscular tension decreases, your nervous system shifts toward regulation. Awareness becomes less reactive and more active.

The room itself has not changed, rather what has shifted is the condition of the instrument perceiving it.

Notes.

INTEGRATION PRACTICE 4
Place Awareness

For the next week:

1. Focus your attention to the "weather" of each room using two or three descriptors.
2. Pause briefly at thresholds and notice what shifts as your attention moves.
3. Observe where your body naturally relaxes without effort.

Place awareness becomes essential later, particularly when navigating shared environments, emotional spaces, and boundaries.

Observations.

Closing Thought

Places register movement, use, and tone.

They may support or drain, soften or sharpen, without a word being spoken.

When you notice rooms in this way, you are not adding a new skill. You are restoring a perceptual capacity that modern life often leaves unattended.

Your organismic intelligence has always responded to space.

Now your active awareness is present for that responsiveness.

There is a common belief that clear perception requires time to "warm up," as though awareness must slowly gather itself before anything can register.

That may appear true in settings where attention is scattered or ritualized. But when attention is steady and directed, clear perception does not arrive gradually.

Again and again, I noticed that the moment my attention focused on what was being sensed, the impression was already there.

No delay. No buildup. Just immediate registration.

— Adapted from Ingo Swann, *Remote Viewing: The Real Story*

Notes.

5 | Attention & Connection
Presence Before Words or Touch

Opening Invitation

Up to this point, perception has been explored in sections: internal sensation, near-body space, shared atmosphere, and the architecture of rooms.

This chapter turns to one of the central principles of organismic intelligence: attention shapes relationship through orientation rather than through effort or intention.

Attention is often treated as mental focus alone. In lived experience, however, attention is relational. Where attention turns, the body adjusts:

Sensation shifts. → Posture changes. → Readiness increases. → Connection begins to form (often before words, gestures, or physical contact).

When attention moves, something in you moves with it. No force is required. This is how it organizes itself in relation to others.

We already understand this inferentially. Common expressions reflect this:

- ⟩ give me your attention
- ⟩ pay attention
- ⟩ full attention
- ⟩ they're just looking for attention
- ⟩ this needs your attention
- ⟩ don't draw attention to it

These phrases reveal that attention is experienced as active and directional. It can be given, withheld, divided, or drawn. Long before we analyze it, we recognize that attention connects (or disconnects) us from what surrounds us.

This chapter explores attention as the first point of engagement: how presence forms, how connection begins, and how awareness participates in relationship before touch or speech.

 **The Many Domains of Attention**

In lived experience, attention does not operate in a single way. It functions across several overlapping domains:

1. **Attention as Focus:** directing awareness toward one thing ("Give me your attention.")
2. **Attention as Resource:** sustaining or dividing capacity ("I can't split my attention right now.")
3. **Attention as Social Recognition:** acknowledgment or visibility ("They just want attention.")
4. **Attention as Alertness:** readiness or orientation ("Attention!")
5. **Attention as Care:** tending, maintaining, or supporting ("This needs attention.")
6. **Attention as Currency:** something given, withheld, or spent ("That's worth my attention.")
7. **Attention as Valuation:** weighting and prioritizing signals ("What you attend to grows.")

These are not abstract categories. They describe how your perceptual awareness system participates with others and with space, and more so how attention moves, allocates, responds, and connects in everyday life.

When attention assigns weight, it also orients.

Attention as Engagement

Where you place your attention, relationship begins. Even lightly, this initiates:

⟩ a point of contact
⟩ a channel for information
⟩ a shift in tone or pressure
⟩ a change in how you and the other orient to one another

This is not control or influence. It is participation. Attention is an organismic response. It is how organismic perception leans toward what matters.

Each time your attention orients, something in you adjusts toward what you are noticing. Connection forms, before intention, before action, and often before you are aware it has happened.

Exploring the Domains of Attention in Your Own Language

Take a moment to write down three phrases you use or hear regularly that include the word attention.

Examples:

> Give me your attention.
> I can't divide my attention right now.
> This deserves my attention.

For each phrase, ask:

Which domain does this reflect?

> Focus?
> Resource?
> Social recognition?
> Alertness?
> Care?
> Currency?
> Valuation?

Notice how the same word points to different lived experiences depending on context.

These domains describe how attention is discussed and applied.

Later, you will explore how attention behaves in perception itself, how it moves, settles, connects, and withdraws before words are involved.

How Attention Behaves

In lived perception, attention does not operate as a single function.

It shifts between distinct modes depending on context and relationship:

1. Selective attention: highlights one signal over others.
2. Divided attention: monitors multiple signals at once.
3. Sustained attention: remains with something over time.
4. Orienting attention: turns toward change, movement, or approach.
5. Open attention: softens and receives without selecting.
6. Withdrawn attention: turns inward, reducing external engagement.

These modes are not learned concepts.

They appear long before formal reasoning.

You demonstrate them every day:

> turning toward a sudden sound (orienting)
> tracking both a conversation and the room around you (divided)
> reading steadily without strain (sustained)

You do not need physical contact to register someone's presence.

You do not need reasoning to sense mood.

You do not need visual focus to notice attention directed toward you.

Attention organizes information first.

Notes.

EXPLORATION 5.1: Spotlight Mode vs. Lantern Mode
Two Modes of Attention, Two Distinct Effects

Objective

To notice the difference between narrow, concentrated attention and diffuse, open attention.

Setup

Sit in a room with several objects. Feet grounded. Eyes open or gently closed.

Steps

1. Choose one object and focus tightly on it, like a spotlight concentrating light into a single beam. (Spotlight Mode)
   → Let everything else recede into the background.
2. Notice what happens in your body.
3. Release your focus.
4. Widen your attention until you register the whole room at once, like a lantern spreading light evenly in all directions. (Lantern Mode)
   → Do not search or scan. Let what you are aware of become panoramic, inclusive rather than selective.
5. Compare the two modes.

What to Watch For

⟩ spotlight: narrow, sharp, effortful, tense
⟩ lantern: open, relaxed, spacious, warm

Reflection

↺ Which mode felt more natural to notice?
↺ Which felt more effortful to sustain?

Why This Matters

Attention is not only focus. It is an active force that shapes how your presence engages with others and with space:

> Spotlight Mode attention concentrates and presses outward.
> Lantern Mode attention softens and expands.

Becoming aware of which mode you are using clarifies how your presence influences the environment you're in.

Notes.

EXPLORATION 5.2: Split Attention

Holding More Than One Perceptual Point at Once

Objective

To experience your attention resting in more than one place at the same time.

Setup

Choose a quiet location where you can remain still for a few minutes. Sit or stand comfortably.

Steps

1. Focus your attention on your breath or heartbeat.
2. Allow this internal point to remain steady without forcing it.
3. Without losing that internal anchor, widen your attention to include the space around you.
4. Let the room remain in your awareness while your breath continues in the background.
5. Hold both points lightly: the internal rhythm and the surrounding space.
6. Notice how your attention moves between them without fully abandoning either.
7. After a short time, release the external point and return fully to your breath.
8. Then release your breath and allow your attention to rest in the room alone.

What to Watch For

> your attention widening or stretching
> shifts in bodily sensation as your attention expands
> asymmetrical pressure or spatial orientation
> moments where both points feel present at once

Reflection

↺ Which point held your attention more easily: the internal anchor or the surrounding space?
↺ Did your attention move back and forth between the two points, or did they remain present together?
↺ Did holding two points feel steady, stretched, or unstable?

Why This Happens

Attention is flexible. It can narrow toward a single point or widen to include multiple locations at once.

Attention can divide, but awareness maintains the span. When your body is regulated and steady, the two work together to hold more than one perceptual point at a time.

This relationship becomes important in later explorations, where you remain grounded internally while also registering what is occurring around you.

Notes.

EXPLORATION 5.3: Distant Attention
Relational Noticing Across Space

Objective

To notice how your attention can activate relational memory and bodily response even when another person is not physically present.

Setup

Sit comfortably in a quiet environment. Allow your feet to remain grounded and your shoulders relaxed. Your eyes may remain open or gently closed. Take a moment to notice your current internal state before beginning.

Steps

1. Bring to mind someone you know well.
2. Do not visualize them in detail. Simply allow the sense of that person to enter your awareness.
3. Notice whether anything shifts in your body as your attention turns toward them.
4. Allow your attention to rest lightly on this relational presence.
5. Observe any changes in sensation, posture, breath, or emotional tone.
6. After a short time, release your attention and allow your awareness to return fully to yourself.
7. Notice how your internal state changes after your attention is released.

What to Watch For

> pull, push, or neutrality
> warmth, coolness or temperature shifts
> small adjustments in your posture or muscle tone
> a shift in your emotional tone or mood

Reflection

↻ What changed in your body as your attention moved toward the person?
↻ How did the sensation differ before, during, and after?
↻ What was more noticeable: sensation, tone, or orientation?
↻ Did the experience feel more physical, emotional, or spatial?

Why This Happens

Attention engages an internal relational map shaped by lived experience. When your attention turns toward someone familiar, aspects of that pattern may briefly reappear. Your body recalls the relationship through shifts in tone, orientation, and internal sensation.

This map is sensory before it is conceptual. It quietly organizes how you attend, respond, and connect.

Notes.

EXPLORATION 5.4: Closing the Circuit
Withdrawing Attention

Objective

To deliberately withdraw your attention from an external focus and restore internal coherence.

Setup

Sit comfortably in a neutral environment. Feet grounded. Eyes open or gently closed.

Steps

1. Bring to mind a person or situation that has been occupying your attention.
   → Do not analyze it. Simply allow it to register briefly.
2. Notice what changes in your body. (Where does tension appear? Does posture shift? Does breath alter?)
3. Now, instead of continuing to engage, redirect attention to your own physical presence.
   → Feel your feet.
   → Feel your hands.
   → Feel the weight of your body supported.
4. Inhale slowly and allow your attention to gather toward the center of your body (chest, belly, or spine).
5. Exhale and allow your attention to settle fully within your own body.
6. Let the image or situation fade into the background without forcing it away.

What to Watch For

〉 your jaw, shoulders, or abdomen releasing
〉 your breath deepening or lengthening
〉 emotional quiet or neutrality returning

Reflection

↺ How does your body feel when your attention returns to you?
↺ What changed as your attention moved away from the person or situation?
↺ Did tension reduce, shift, or remain present?

Why Closing Matters

Attention forms relational links. When your attention remains directed outward, your body maintains readiness in response to what it is oriented toward. Unclosed attention can lead to:

> fatigue
> emotional leakage
> confusion
> overwhelm

Closing the circuit restores clarity and containment.

Notes.

How Attention Behaves in Relationships

In this chapter, you explored attention as something that can:

⟩ narrow
⟩ widen
⟩ divide
⟩ extend
⟩ connect
⟩ withdraw

Attention is not static. It shifts, organizes, and responds.

Where attention moves, relationship begins to form.

Where attention returns, coherence reestablishes.

INTEGRATION PRACTICE 5
The Daily Attention Check

Ask yourself 2–3 times a day:

1. Where is my attention (or focus) right now?
2. Is it narrow or open?
3. Is it anchored or drifting?
4. What changes when I return attention (or focus) to presence in my body for ten seconds?

This brief check can restore presence.

Observations.

Closing Thought

Attention is one of the simplest (and most powerful) forms of relational perception.

We speak about it constantly without realizing what we are describing:

> we pull someone's attention
> we command attention
> we cling to someone's attention
> we lose attention and drift
> we split attention and weaken contact
> we withdraw attention and reclaim ourselves
> we give attention as care
> we pay attention as if it has value
> we attract attention unintentionally
> we avoid attention when vulnerable
> we demand attention in urgency
> we capture attention through presence
> we hold attention through connection
> we drop attention to close a circuit

Our everyday expressions treat attention as a dynamic force:

> movement
> exchange
> value
> boundary
> contact
> force

Because that is how attention behaves in lived experience:

> Where attention goes, connection forms.
> Where attention softens, space opens.
> Where attention returns, sovereignty restores.

6 | The Touchless Handshake
Being in Another Person's Presence Without Physical Contact

Opening Invitation

A person's presence is not confined to the boundary of their skin.

Long before someone speaks, smiles, or moves closer, something in you is already responding, through shifts in attention, emotional tone, breath, posture, and changes in orientation. These adjustments occur quietly, often before reflective thought.

Ingo noted this responsiveness appears early in life. Infants orient toward people before language or reasoning are available. Their attention shifts. Their bodies adjust. Their state changes. Anyone who has spent time with young children has seen this: a baby turning toward someone entering the room, settling or tensing before physical contact occurs.

This reflects a basic feature of human perception:

〉 proximity detected before sight fully engages
〉 emotional tone sensed before words are spoken
〉 presence detected before interpretation begins

This chapter is not about rooms or environments. It is about relationship; specifically, how two perceptual awareness systems encounter one another prior to touch or speech:

〉 two bodies orienting
〉 two systems adjusting
〉 two patterns of attention meeting

You do not need to see someone to notice their approach. You do not need physical contact to sense interest, hesitation, or withdrawal. You are organized to become aware of presence and proximity before your intellect assigns meaning.

This is the touchless handshake. It is the quiet moment of mutual orientation that precedes words.

This chapter invites you to notice that exchange clearly and steadily, without strain or projection.

Note: If at any point an exercise feels uncomfortable, stop. Organismic perception includes choice, boundaries, and self-respect.

EXPLORATION 6.1: The Behind-You Effect
When the Body Registers Someone Nearby

Objective

To observe the moment another person's presence is registered without relying on sight or sound.

Setup

Work with a trusted partner. Choose a quiet, familiar space where footsteps are unlikely to be heard.

Steps

1. Sit or stand facing away from your partner.
2. Soften your gaze or gently close your eyes.
3. Ask your partner to begin 10–15 feet behind you.
4. Your partner walks slowly and quietly toward you at a steady pace.
5. At the moment you sense their presence, say "stop."
6. After stopping, notice the distance between you and compare it with the moment you registered their presence.

What to Watch For

> a sense of pressure or orientation behind you
> warmth, alertness, or readiness rising
> tingling or a small posture shift
> your breath responding before thought
> simple internal recognition: *someone is here*

Reflection

↺ What registered first: sensation, breath, posture, or orientation?
↺ How did the moment of recognition feel in your body?
↺ Did the recognition appear suddenly or gradually?
↺ What changed in your body after your partner stopped moving?

Why This Happens

This exploration draws on several overlapping processes:

> sensory receptors responding to subtle changes in air movement and pressure
> your body's bioelectrical activity adjusting in response to proximity
> evolutionary orientation systems that monitor approach and distance
> pre-conscious processing of movement, presence, and potential contact

Together, these processes allow you to notice approach before your intellect evaluates what is happening.

Notes.

EXPLORATION 6.2: The Side-Sweep Effect

Presence in Peripheral Space

Objective

To notice what emerges as your attention extends across your peripheral space.

Setup

Work with a trusted partner in a quiet, open space where footsteps are unlikely to be heard.

Steps

1. Face forward with a soft, relaxed gaze.
2. Ask your partner to begin a few feet behind you.
3. Your partner slowly walks in an arc around your body, moving quietly so their footsteps are not audible.
4. As they move toward one side of your peripheral space, say "now" the moment you detect their presence, even if you cannot see them clearly.
5. Pause briefly afterward and notice what remains in your body.
6. Return to the starting position and repeat the process from the other side.

What to Watch For

> one side registering sooner than the other
> a wave-like or directional internal movement
> shifts in your breath, chest, or posture
> a quiet change in emotional tone (these responses may be faint or asymmetrical)

Reflection

↺ How did your body register movement across your sides?
↺ Did one side respond sooner or more markedly?
↺ What shifted as presence moved from one side to the other?
↺ Did your breath, posture, or internal tone change during the movement?

Why This Matters

Your system continuously monitors the space around you, including areas outside your direct line of sight. Subtle changes in movement, airflow, sound, and spatial orientation can register in the body before they become fully visible or consciously interpreted.

Many people notice differences in how their bodies register presence laterally. These variations are not problems to correct. They are simply information about how your system distributes attention and orientation around your body.

Notes.

EXPLORATION 6.3: The Hand Hover Effect
Near-Body Interaction Without Touch

Objective

To notice how two bodies register one another in close proximity without physical contact.

Setup

Sit or stand facing a trusted partner in a comfortable, neutral posture.

Steps

1. Extend one hand comfortably in front of you.
2. Your partner brings their hand to within 4–6 inches of yours, without touching.
3. Soften your gaze or gently close your eyes.
4. Ask your partner to move their hand slightly closer and farther away, staying within that range.
5. Notice how your body responds as the distance between your hands changes.
6. Switch roles and repeat.

What to Watch For

〉 warmth or coolness between the hands
〉 pulsing, buzzing, or tingling
〉 pressure or resistance (sensations may be faint, uneven, or brief)
〉 a shift in emotional tone
〉 a sense of approach or withdrawal

Reflection

↺ How did the space between your hands register through sensation?
↺ Did the sensation change as the distance between your hands shifted?
↺ Did anything change as your attention steadied or moved?
↺ Did the experience feel directional, symmetrical, or uneven?
↺ What aspect of the interaction felt most distinct?

Why This Happens

Human physiological systems are socially and environmentally responsive.

Internal regulation shifts in shared environments: stress hormones adjust, sleep-wake cycles influence one another, emotional tone shapes autonomic balance, and nervous systems attune through proximity and routine.

The key principle is not synchronization, rather mutual regulation and sensitivity.

Many internal rhythms (including menstrual cycles) are hormonally regulated and responsive to stress, safety, routine, and circadian influences. When people live closely together, shared context can shape internal regulation even without precise alignment.

Your body adjusts to conditions before your intellect explains why.

Notes.

EXPLORATION 6.4: The Approach Line
Calibrating Personal Space

Objective

To notice how your organismic intelligence regulates near-body (peripersonal) space, signaling connection, readiness, or "enough" as personal space expands or contracts.

Setup

Stand with a trusted partner in a quiet, open space.

Steps

1. Stand facing each other about 10 feet apart.
2. Ask your partner to walk slowly toward you.
3. Say "stop" at the moment you first detect:
   - → alertness
   - → pressure
   - → an emotional shift
   - → a feeling of "too close" or discomfort
4. Note the distance.
5. Repeat the exercise with different approaches:
   - → front
   - → side
   - → behind
   - → diagonal
6. Pause briefly between rounds.

What to Watch For

> differences depending on direction of approach
> boundaries expanding when you feel calm or confident
> boundaries contracting under stress or fatigue
> an emotional tone influencing when "enough" is signaled

Reflection

↺ When did you first notice a change in your internal state?
↺ At what distance did your system signal "enough"?

Why This Happens

Human beings continuously regulate interpersonal distance. As someone approaches, your perceptual awareness system evaluates:

> distance
> direction of approach
> speed
> posture and tone
> your own internal state

Your body adjusts before conscious thought. Your muscle tone shifts, breath changes, and alertness increases or softens.

Notes.

INTEGRATION PRACTICE 6
Presence Sensing

Throughout the week:

1. Notice when someone enters your awareness before you see them.
2. Track how close strangers can approach before your body or attention shifts.
3. Direct your attention to emotional tone directly, without analyzing or explaining it.
4. Compare forward-facing awareness with awareness behind you.

These moments provide an opportunity to build trust in how you naturally record proximity, presence, and change.

Observations.

Closing Thought

Presence is relational.

It is detected through proximity, tone, and attention, not touch.

> You do not need eyes to become aware of someone nearby.
> You do not need logic to sense mood.
> You do not need contact to feel connection.

You already do this. This chapter simply brings the process into your awareness.

Next, we turn to nature... the purest model of perceptual coherence.

7 | Natural Feedback
Using Trees, Wind, Water, & Open Space to Clarify Perception

Opening Invitation

Nature is the most coherent context for perception.

Long before cities and screens, human awareness evolved in continuous interaction with wind, trees, water, and open sky.

Our capacity to be aware of movement, pressure, safety, openness, and direction developed outdoors, in environments that offered constant sensory feedback rather than constant stimulation.

Ingo understood this directly. As a boy, after an emotionally painful moment in church, he stepped outside and stood before a towering pine tree. Its presence offered no words, yet something in him rebalanced.

The charge of embarrassment softened, his breath slowed and his body steadied.

The contrast between the dense emotional atmosphere indoors and the steady presence of the tree produced a shift. It did not happen through interpretation, but instead through perception.

His attention moved. And as it moved, relationship formed.

The tree did not act on him. He oriented toward it. In that orientation, his body adjusted. Readiness changed. Emotional tone recalibrated. Presence reorganized.

This is how attention shapes connection: before words, before touch, before intention.

Years later, when he shared the experience with the woman involved, she admitted she too had often spent time with that tree. Neither meant literal conversation. They were naming a felt interaction: the way a living environment can stabilize attention, absorb excess activation, and support nervous-system regulation through contrast and consistency.

Modern terminology might describe this as interoceptive regulation, environmental contrast, or autonomic settling.

Natural environments often provide a form of perceptual grounding that many human-built spaces do not, something Ingo recognized in his own reflections.

This chapter explores that same dynamic: how trees, wind, water, and open space clarify perception, reveal internal state through contrast, and allow your awareness to return to coherence without effort.

Nature does not require interpretation. It offers stable conditions.

Your system does the rest.

Note: If at any point an exploration feels destabilizing, pause and return attention to breath, posture, or physical contact with the ground. Organismic perception always includes choice and self-regulation.

EXPLORATION 7.1: The Tree Proximity Effect
Living Systems Registering Without Touch

Objective

To notice how a living plant or tree is registered through organismic perception without physical contact.

Setup

Stand in a calm outdoor space.

Choose a tree or large plant that feels neutral or comfortable.

Steps

1. Move within 2–4 feet from the trunk or main body of the tree.
2. Soften or close your eyes.
3. Extend one hand toward the tree at a comfortable height.
4. Move your hand slowly through the space near the bark.
5. Adjust the distance slightly and notice what changes.
6. Move slowly. There is no need to search for sensation.

What to Watch For

> warmth or coolness
> stillness or subtle movement
> a sense of density or openness near the surface
> an evident boundary where sensation shifts
> an overall quality of steadiness or groundedness

Reflection

↺ What qualities stood out most freely?
↺ How did this differ from your experience with non-living materials in Exploration 3.3?
↺ How did your body register those differences?

Why Trees Register Strongly

Trees are continuously active biological systems. Water moves upward, electrical gradients shift, and chemical processes operate without pause. These forms of organized activity create stable sensory conditions that human perception can register as steadiness, density, or presence, without touch and without interpretation.

Organismic perception often registers this kind of organization before conscious explanation arises.

Notes.

EXPLORATION 7.2: The Wind Response
Movement as Relational Input

Objective

To observe how moving air influences organismic perception beyond surface sensation.

Setup

Go outside on a day with light to moderate wind. Choose a place where you can stand comfortably without distraction.

Steps

1. Stand still with your eyes softened or gently closed.
2. Notice the wind contacting your skin.
3. Then notice how your internal state responds.
4. Slowly move your hands through the air and observe any changes.
5. Stay with simple noticing. There is no need to interpret what you feel.

What to Watch For

> heightened sensitivity in certain areas of your body
> emotional shifts
> changes in your breath, posture, or readiness
> your awareness widening or narrowing

Reflection

> What changed in your body as the wind moved?
> How did your breath, posture, or attention respond?
> What differed between still air and moving air?
> How would you describe the quality of the wind as it registered in your body (lifting, sharp, calming, unsettling)?
> How did variations in movement or unpredictability influence your internal state?

Why Wind Matters

Wind makes perceptual contrast immediately noticeable.

As conditions shift, you may notice differences between:

〉 tight and open states
〉 regulated and agitated responses
〉 narrowed and widened attention

Because wind is variable and unpredictable, it provides clear feedback about how coherence holds (or loosens) under changing conditions.

Information often becomes noticeable through contrast.

Notes.

EXPLORATION 7.3: The Water Sensitivity Effect
Water's Influence

Objective

To notice how proximity to water influences your attention, breath, and internal tone.

Setup

Sit or stand near water: natural (river, lake, ocean) or contained (fountain, bowl).

Steps

1. Soften your gaze or gently close your eyes.
2. Notice the surrounding space.
3. Observe how your breath responds.
4. Extend one hand toward the water at a comfortable distance.
5. Remain still long enough for your attention to orient. There is no need to reach for a particular experience.

What to Watch For

> cooling or settling sensations
> emotional softening or quieting
> awareness of rhythmic movement
> a gentle inward draw of your attention
> reduced mental activity or background noise (responses may be subtle and gradual)

Reflection

↺ What changed as you remained near the water?
↺ How did your breath, attention, or internal tone shift over time?
↺ What felt most distinct compared to still, dry space?

Why Water Matters

Water environments often support regulation through multiple factors:

> conductive properties
> rhythmic movement
> thermal influence
> resonance with the body's own fluid composition

These conditions tend to support steadier breath, softened attention, and reduced internal interference, not because water "induces" calm, but because your nervous system responds to consistency, rhythm, and temperature.

Your body recognizes supportive conditions before your intellect names them.

Notes.

EXPLORATION 7.4: Nature Coherence Check
Environmental Contrast & Regulation

Objective

To notice how natural environments help clarify your internal state through contrast and regulation.

Setup

Choose any natural setting where you can sit or stand comfortably (forest, park, shoreline, open field, or garden).

Steps

1. Sit or stand in a relaxed posture.
2. Notice the surrounding environment without naming or evaluating it.
3. Notice your body within that environment.
4. Gently compare internal qualities such as:
   - → heavy / light
   - → open / closed
   - → calm / agitated
5. Allow a few moments between comparisons.

What to Watch For

> your breath naturally slowing or deepening
> your muscles releasing without effort
> your attention widening or stabilizing
> your emotional tone becoming quieter or more well-defined (changes may occur gradually rather than all at once)

Reflection

↺ What became more apparent about your internal state as you stayed with the landscape?

↺ Did any contrasts stand out between your body and the surrounding environment?

↺ What shifted without effort or intention?

Why Nature Matters

Natural environments provide patterned, non-demanding sensory input:

> variable but coherent light
> layered, non-abrupt sound
> fractal visual structure
> organic movement and spatial variation

These differ from the concentrated, repetitive, and high-intensity stimuli typical of modern built environments.

Such patterned variability has been shown to:

> place less strain on directed attention
> reduce cognitive load
> support autonomic regulation
> allow breath and muscular tone to relax

Natural settings can therefore function as calibration environments. They do not impose a particular state; they make your current state easier to perceive.

The contrast allows you to distinguish what belongs to the environment and what belongs to you.

Notes.

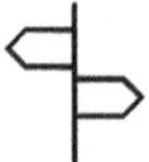

Coherence in Living Systems

Earlier, coherence was introduced as the condition in which body, nervous system, attention, and perception operate in alignment rather than in competition.

Here, that idea is extended.

In living systems, coherence is not something that is created or imposed. It emerges when unnecessary interference is reduced.

Breath, sensation, emotional tone, and awareness begin to move together. Responses become more economical and you system stabilizes without strain.

This pattern is not unique to humans. It is a fundamental property of life.

Natural systems demonstrate coherence continuously:

> trees regulate moisture and energy through coordinated internal exchange
> animal nervous systems cycle predictably between activation and rest
> ecosystems adjust through feedback rather than force

These systems do not strive for coherence. They maintain it by responding accurately to conditions.

When human systems are immersed in environments organized this way, attention and physiology often reorganize naturally. Noise drops, rhythm returns, and what you notice clarifies.

Nature does not produce coherence or teach it.

It provides conditions in which coherence becomes the most efficient state.

INTEGRATION PRACTICE 7
Nature as Calibration

This week, spend brief periods in natural environments and notice what changes.

> approach living systems slowly
> attend to movement, rhythm, and steadiness
> allow breath and attention to reorganize

Notice when what you are aware of becomes distinctive without effort.

Observations.

Closing Thought

You are not separate from nature; you are continuous with it.

Trees, wind, water, and your own body operate under the same organizing principles.

When you spend time in natural conditions, your system often steadies and mental clutter diminishes.

It does this not through instruction, but through regulation.

Nature does not teach or direct.

- ⟩ It provides stable conditions.
- ⟩ It does not impose.
- ⟩ It allows recalibration.

In these conditions, what you notice tends to become more discernible, and more reliable. This is not because anything is added, but because interference drops.

What remains is coherence.

8 | Perceptual Maintenance
Clearing, Grounding, & Resetting

Opening Invitation

Most people recognize the relief that follows rain.

The air feels lighter. Breathing becomes easier. The atmosphere shifts without effort.

Storms disperse accumulated charge, move stagnant air, and restore circulation. Living systems respond to that change immediately. When the environment clears, the body exhales, attention steadies, and tone shifts.

Your organismic intelligence works in much the same way.

Across an ordinary day, perceptual load accumulates:

> emotional tone from others
> environmental stress
> digital saturation
> sensory overload
> unprocessed internal states

None of this arrives dramatically. It gathers gradually, the way humidity builds before a storm.

Living organisms operate through electrical, chemical, and regulatory processes. Long before this was described in modern terms, people recognized this through lived experience. Contemporary physiology now confirms what early observation suggested:

> nerves communicate through electrical impulses
> muscles contract through changes in voltage
> heart rhythms generate measurable electromagnetic activity
> skin conductivity shifts with emotional state
> grounding alters charge distribution within tissues

Ingo sensed these dynamics organically and painted them.

In one such work, a calm, centered face is surrounded by turbulent bands of color: stillness held within activation.

He rendered visually what many people recognize somatically: charge, residue, and release.

We may not see these shifts directly, but we feel them:

> heaviness after crowded spaces
> relief when stepping outdoors
> the settling effect of water
> the stabilizing influence of connection with the ground

Just as weather clears the atmosphere, our systems sometimes needs clearing as well.

This is not purification or ritual. It is maintenance.

> Grounding stabilizes.
> Breath synchronizes.
> Water supports reset.
> Attention re-centers.
> Clearing restores clarity.

You care for your body.

You care for your home.

You clear your inbox.

You benefit from the same uncomplicated attention.

When perceptual maintenance is regular, clarity increases, reactivity decreases, and experience becomes easier to navigate.

You remain oriented rather than carrying everything you have absorbed.

EXPLORATION 8.1: The Grounding Drop
Stabilizing Activation Through Physical Support

When stress or emotional load accumulates, grounding offers a simple way to reduce activation and allow your internal systems to reorganize.

Objective

To reduce excess activation and restore your internal stability through physical contact and posture.

Setup

Stand barefoot or in thin-soled shoes on a solid, supportive surface.

Steps

1. Stand with your feet about hip-width apart.
2. Inhale slowly through your nose.
3. On the exhale, allow your weight to settle downward into your feet.
4. Soften your knees, jaw, and shoulders.
5. Remain for about 30 seconds, breathing naturally.
6. There is no need to force relaxation. Let your body adjust.

What to Watch For

> your breath deepening or slowing
> your legs warming or feeling heavier
> your shoulders lowering
> your mental activity quieting
> a felt sense of "dropping" into the body (attention shifting from thought toward physical sensation... this response may be gradual rather than immediate)

Reflection

↻ Did your internal state shift?
↻ What changed as your weight moved downward?
↻ Did your sense of stability increase?

Why This Happens

Physical connection with stable surfaces provides a tactile reference for posture, balance, and orientation. Grounding supports regulation by:

> reducing excess activation
> calming autonomic arousal
> stabilizing emotional tone
> strengthening physical orientation
> helping your system return to baseline

This is not a special technique. It is a basic regulatory skill, simple, repeatable, and effective because it works with your body's existing processes of self-regulation.

Notes.

EXPLORATION 8.2: The Breath Sweep

Using Exhalation to Support Regulation

Earlier exercises introduced breath regulation. This exploration uses the breath slightly differently.

Objective

To support perceptual reset by allowing the exhale to release accumulated tension and restore internal steadiness.

Setup

Sit or stand in a comfortable, supported posture.

Steps

1. Inhale slowly through your nose for 4 seconds.
2. Exhale through your mouth for 6 seconds.
3. As you exhale, allow your attention to move downward through your body, from your chest to your belly to your legs.
4. Let the exhale feel releasing rather than forced.
5. Repeat for 5–10 breath cycles.
6. Allow the rhythm to remain easy. The quality of your breath matters more than the count.

What to Watch For

> a feeling of lightness or space in your body
> tingling or warmth as tension releases
> reduced muscular holding in your shoulders, jaw, or belly
> emotional softening or neutralization
> quieter or clearer mental activity

Reflection

↺ How did your internal state change across several breaths?
↺ Did tension shift downward or release during the exhale?
↺ Did your body feel clearer or lighter afterward?
↺ Did today's response differ from previous experiences?

Why This Happens

Extended exhalation engages regulatory pathways that support calming and integration. As your breath slows and lengthens, your muscular tension often releases, emotional tone steadies, and perceptual interference reduces.

Breath does not erase experience.

It allows your system to reorganize how experience is held.

Notes.

EXPLORATION 8.3: The Hand Sweep
Recalibrating Near-Body Awareness

Objective

To reduce lingering activation near your body and restore a sense of boundary and orientation.

Setup

Sit or stand in a comfortable, upright posture.

Steps

1. Hold your hands a few inches away from your body.
2. Let your attention remain light. There is no need to visualize or imagine anything.
3. Slowly sweep downward from head to feet without touching the skin.
4. After each pass, gently shake or relax your hands.
5. Repeat 3–5 times, moving at an unhurried pace.

What to Watch For

> a feeling of release or lightness
> warmth dispersing or shifting
> increased spaciousness near your body
> a quieting of your mental or emotional activity

Reflection

↺ Where did the sensation or activation feel most concentrated?
↺ How did the sensations vary in intensity or location?
↺ What shifted as you repeated the sweep?

Why This Happens

Awareness does not stop at your skin. Your body continuously monitors near-body space through posture, movement, and spatial sensing.

Slow, deliberate sweeping movements:

> reestablish awareness of bodily boundaries
> reduce residual muscular and attentional tension
> engage spatial orientation systems
> signal the nervous system to reset

The effect is often faint rather than dramatic.

Clarity increases as unnecessary activation releases.

Notes.

EXPLORATION 8.4: The Water Reset
Using Water to Regulate Activation & Restore Coherence

Objective

To allow emotional and perceptual load to decrease through engagement with water.

Setup

Use a sink, shower, bath, or natural water source, whatever is readily available.

Steps

1. Run your hands under flowing water.
2. Stay with the sensation without distraction.
3. If showering, allow the water to fall across your upper back and shoulders.
4. Remain for 10–20 seconds, breathing naturally (there is no need to seek a particular effect).

What to Watch For

> your emotional tone shifting
> your breath easing or deepening
> your muscular tension releasing
> a general sense of lightening or reset (changes may be subtle rather than dramatic)

Reflection

↺ How did interaction with water influence your internal state?
↺ What shifted as you remained with the flow?

Why This Happens

Water environments tend to support regulation through several factors:

> conductive properties
> rhythmic movement and flow
> thermal influence
> resonance with the body's predominantly fluid composition

These conditions often make it easier for you to return to perceptual coherence. This is why people instinctively wash after periods of intensity. It is not as a ritual, but as a practical reset.

Water does not remove experience.

It supports your body in allowing excess activation to resolve.

Notes.

EXPLORATION 8.5: The Quick Gather

Restoring Containment After Openness

Objective

To return your attention to a stable, contained state after an interaction, observation, or environmental exposure.

Setup

Anywhere. This practice is designed to be brief and portable.

Steps

1. Pause wherever you are and bring your attention back toward your body.
2. Notice your feet, hands, or the weight of your body being supported.
3. Take a slow, unforced breath.
4. As you exhale, allow your attention to gather closer to your physical center (chest, belly, or spine).
5. Let your shoulders soften and your jaw release.
6. Notice the space immediately around you becoming more defined.

What to Watch For

> a feeling of calm returning
> reduced internal noise / mental activity
> a clearer sense of your own physical boundaries
> a quiet sense of completion or reset

Reflection

↺ What shifted as you gathered your attention back toward yourself?
↺ Did your physical boundaries feel clearer or more defined?
↺ How quickly did the reset occur?

The Function of Containment

Openness supports organismic intelligence, but continuous openness is not sustainable.

Without moments of closure, your organismic intelligence can become:

> fatigued
> emotionally diffuse
> less discriminating
> less clearly oriented

Brief acts of gathering restore balance. They allow your attention, sensation, and emotional tone to come back into alignment, supporting perceptual coherence and self-presence.

Containment is not withdrawal.

It is how openness remains usable.

Notes.

INTEGRATION PRACTICE 8
Daily Perceptual Maintenance

Each day, choose one or two practices based on context and need:

> **Morning:** Grounding Drop (to establish stability)
> **Midday:** Hand Sweep (to reduce accumulated activation)
> **Evening:** Water Release (to support regulation and recalibration)
> **Quick:** Gather (to restore containment after openness)

These practices are not meant to be performed rigidly or all at once. Used briefly and consistently, they can help prevent overload and support clarity over time.

Regulation works best when it is simple, responsive, and repeatable.

Observations.

Closing Thought

Clarity isn't rare. It's maintained.

Your organismic intelligence is living. It responds, accumulates, and resets.

What keeps your system trustworthy is not intensity, but care.

1. **Grounding** steadies.
2. **Clearing** refreshes.
3. **Containment** preserves orientation and self-presence.

Perceptual maintenance is not improvement.

It is upkeep.

And upkeep is what makes the process sustainable.

You are not making yourself more sensitive.

You are keeping your instrument clear enough to notice what has been there all along.

CODA

WHAT HAS COME BACK INTO VIEW

Opening Invitation

You began this book not by trying to become more perceptive, but by noticing what was already happening:

> rooms carrying emotional weather
> people adjusting when attention touched them
> your body registering pressure, distance, and tone
> nature settling you without instruction
> simple maintenance practices clearing perceptual load

You've discovered that perception is not an abstract talent. It is something you are doing all the time.

This book did not ask you to add anything new. You slowed down enough to recognize what was already there.

What You Have Already Reclaimed

Across these chapters you have:

1. **Reopened basic awareness.**
   Re-established engagement with your internal sensation, breath, and near-body space.
2. **Noticed relational environment.**
   Seen how groups, rooms, and other people generate atmosphere that your body registers immediately.
3. **Felt attention as connection.**
   Experienced attention as something that narrows, widens, connects, and withdraws, not just "thinking about" something, but touching it.
4. **Used nature as calibration.**
   Let trees, wind, water, and open space show you how your system organizes when conditions are steady.
5. **Navigated through simple upkeep.**
   Grounding, breath, clearing, and gathering: ways to reduce mental interference so information remains usable instead of overwhelming.

All of this is foundation. You have not "become sensitive."

You have become more aware of how perceptive you already were.

Why Noticing Alone Is Not Enough

Noticing is essential, but it is not sufficient.

As perceptual information becomes recognized, you may also have noticed:

> some environments are more draining than others
> some people's presence pulls you off center
> emotional tone lingers after contact
> sensory channels feel more open on some days than others
> increased awareness can feel like "too much" when there is no container

This is where many people either shut perception down or try to push through it.

Book Two takes a different approach.

Rather than striving for more experience, it focuses on how your system holds experience:

> how perceptual coherence forms and weakens
> how emotional texture is read without being swallowed
> how boundaries work as living membranes, not walls

The aim is not greater intensity. The aim is greater stability.

The Pivot into Book Two

Book One asked:

What am I noticing about space, people, and environment?

Book Two begins to ask:

How do I stay steady while all of that is happening?

You will explore:

1. **Perceptual coherence.**
   How breath, posture, attention, and emotional tone come into alignment so the process becomes steadier and less effortful.
2. **Emotional frequency.**
   How emotion functions as texture and tone; as information rather than story, and how to sense it without collapsing into it.
3. **Boundaries.**
   How your natural perimeter signals "enough," how it expands and contracts, and how to let connection happen without losing yourself.

If Book One was about opening your eyes to what is already in motion, Book Two is about standing firmly in yourself while it moves.

Closing Thought

You have already proven something important to yourself:

> your body is a reliable sensing instrument
> your perception extends into space, relationship, and environment
> simple maintenance makes clarity easier, not harder

The next step is not to experience more, but to stand more steadily within what you already experience.

Book Two begins there:

> with perceptual coherence, emotional clarity, and boundaries

They are the supports that make organismic perception sustainable over a lifetime.

APPENDIX

Quick Reset Practices

The brief resets below are not techniques to master or practices to perform regularly. They are simple ways of returning your system to a workable state when it drifts, intensifies, or becomes unclear.

You may use them as needed, or not at all.

Body Reset
(returning to physical presence)

> Exhale longer than you inhale.
> Relax your shoulders.
> Feel a connection to the ground through your feet or seat.
> Drop into the present moment.

Boundary Reset
(restoring perceptual containment)

> Inhale → gently gather your attention to your perimeter.
> Exhale → allow your boundary to close.
> Focus on a soft containment around the body.

Coherence Reset
(stabilizing rhythm and tone)

> Inhale for 5 seconds.
> Exhale for 5 seconds.
> Bring to mind something you appreciate.
> Let your attention smooth and stabilize.

Emotional Check-In
(staying oriented with feeling)

> Where is the sensation located?
> What is its texture?
> What is its direction (up / down / inward / outward)?
> Can it soften with one breath?

Perceptual Reorientation
(returning to balanced attention)

> Turn your attention inward.
> Soften your visual focus.
> Allow your awareness to include the room around you.

SELECTED SCIENTIFIC & PHILOSOPHICAL FOUNDATIONS

The following works have informed the biological, philosophical, and phenomenological perspectives that shape this book.

They are not cited exhaustively, but represent foundational contributions in embodied cognition, interoception, predictive processing, and cross-cultural philosophy of perception.

The explorations in this book draw upon established findings in interoception, peripersonal space, emotional contagion, and autonomic regulation.

They are phenomenological exercises (direct observations of lived experience) grounded in contemporary neuroscience and embodied cognition.

References

Argyle, M., & Cook, M. (1976). *Gaze and mutual gaze*. Cambridge University Press.

Assmann, J. (2001). *Ma'at: Gerechtigkeit und Unsterblichkeit im Alten Ägypten*. C.H. Beck.

Barrett, L. F. (2017). *How emotions are made: The secret life of the brain*. Houghton Mifflin Harcourt.

Becker, R. O., & Selden, G. (1985). *The body electric: Electromagnetism and the foundation of life*. William Morrow.

Blanke, O., & Arzy, S. (2005). The out-of-body experience: Disturbed self-processing at the temporo-parietal junction. *The Neuroscientist, 11*(1), 16–24.

Brozzoli, C., Bolognini, N., Zanini, A., & Farnè, A. (n.d.). *Peripersonal space representation: Neural bases, properties, and functional significance*. In G. J. Boyle, G. Northoff, A. K. Barbey, F. Fregni, M. Jahanshahi, A. Pascual-Leone, & B. J. Sahakian (Eds.), *The SAGE handbook of cognitive and systems neuroscience*.

Clark, A. (2016). *Surfing uncertainty: Prediction, action, and the embodied mind*. Oxford University Press.

Cléry, J., Guipponi, O., Wardak, C., & Ben Hamed, S. (2015). Neuronal bases of peripersonal and extrapersonal spaces, their plasticity and their dynamics: Knowns and unknowns. *Neuropsychologia, 70*, 313–326.

Cifra, M., & Fields, J. Z. (2011). Electromagnetic cellular interactions. *Progress in Biophysics and Molecular Biology, 130*, 197–213.

Conty, L., George, N., & Hietanen, J. K. (2016). Watching eyes effects: When others meet the self. *Consciousness and Cognition, 45*, 184–197.

Craig, A. D. (2002). How do you feel? Interoception: The sense of the physiological condition of the body. *Nature Reviews Neuroscience, 3*(8), 655–666.

Damasio, A. (1999). *The feeling of what happens: Body and emotion in the making of consciousness*. Harcourt Brace.

Damasio, A. (2010). *Self comes to mind: Constructing the conscious brain*. Pantheon Books.

Farb, N. A. S., Segal, Z. V., & Anderson, A. K. (2013). Mindfulness meditation training alters cortical representations of interoceptive attention. *Social Cognitive and Affective Neuroscience, 8*(1), 15–26.

Friston, K. (2010). The free-energy principle: A unified brain theory? *Nature Reviews Neuroscience, 11*(2), 127–138.

Frith, C. D., & Frith, U. (2007). Social cognition in humans. *Current Biology, 17*(16), R724–R732.

Gallagher, S. (2005). *How the body shapes the mind.* Oxford University Press.

Gallese, V. (2005). Embodied simulation: From neurons to phenomenal experience. *Phenomenology and the Cognitive Sciences, 4,* 23–48.

Graziano, M. S. A., & Cooke, D. F. (2006). Parieto-frontal interactions, personal space, and defensive behavior. *Neuropsychologia, 44*(13), 2621–2635.

Haggard, P. (2017). Sense of agency in the human brain. *Nature Reviews Neuroscience, 18*(4), 196–207.

Hatfield, E., Cacioppo, J. T., & Rapson, R. L. (1993). Emotional contagion. *Current Directions in Psychological Science, 2*(3), 96–100.

Hohwy, J. (2013). *The predictive mind.* Oxford University Press.

Kabat-Zinn, J. (1990). *Full catastrophe living.* Delacorte.

Kabat-Zinn, J. (2013). *Full catastrophe living (Revised ed.): Using the wisdom of your body and mind to face stress, pain, and illness.* Bantam Books.

Kahneman, D. (2011). *Thinking, fast and slow.* Farrar, Straus and Giroux.

Khalsa, S. S., Adolphs, R., Cameron, O. G., Critchley, H. D., Davenport, P. W., Feinstein, J. S., et al. (2018). Interoception and mental health: A roadmap. *Biological Psychiatry: Cognitive Neuroscience and Neuroimaging, 3*(6), 501–513.

Lederman, S. J., & Klatzky, R. L. (2009). Haptic perception: A tutorial. *Attention, Perception, & Psychophysics, 71*(7), 1439–1459.

Levin, M. (2014). Molecular bioelectricity in developmental biology: New tools and recent discoveries. *BioEssays, 36*(2), 205–217.

Matilal, B. K. (1986). *Perception: An essay on classical Indian theories of knowledge.* Oxford University Press.

McFadden, J. (2020). Integrating information in the brain's electromagnetic field: The cemi field theory of consciousness. *Neuroscience of Consciousness, 2020*(1), niaa016.

Mehling, W. E., Price, C., Daubenmier, J. J., Acree, M., Bartmess, E., & Stewart, A. (2012). The multidimensional assessment of interoceptive awareness (MAIA). *PLoS ONE, 7*(11), e48230.

Merleau-Ponty, M. (2012). *Phenomenology of perception* (D. A. Landes, Trans.). Routledge. (Original work published 1945)

Noble, D. J., & Hochman, S. (2019). Hypothesis: Pulmonary afferent activity patterns during slow, deep breathing contribute to the neural induction of physiological relaxation. *Frontiers in Physiology, 10*, 1176.

Palumbo, R. V., et al. (2017). Interpersonal autonomic physiology: A systematic review. *Personality and Social Psychology Review, 21*(2), 99–141.

Porges, S. W. (2011). *The polyvagal theory: Neurophysiological foundations of emotions, attachment, communication, and self-regulation.* W. W. Norton.

Rao, R. P. N., & Ballard, D. H. (1999). Predictive coding in the visual cortex: A functional interpretation of some extra-classical receptive-field effects. *Nature Neuroscience, 2*(1), 79–87.

Rivlin, R., & Gravelle, K. (1984). *Deciphering the senses: The expanding world of human perception.* Simon & Schuster.

Rizzolatti, G., Fadiga, L., Fogassi, L., & Gallese, V. (1997). The space around us. *Science, 277*(5323), 190–191.

Rizzolatti, G., & Sinigaglia, C. (2008). *Mirrors in the brain: How our minds share actions and emotions.* Oxford University Press.

Schiffman, H. R. (1976). Sensation and perception: An integrated approach. John Wiley & Sons.

Senju, A., & Johnson, M. H. (2009). The eye contact effect. *Trends in Cognitive Sciences, 13*(3), 127–134.

Serino, A., & Haggard, P. (2010). Space around the body: How the brain represents peripersonal space. *Trends in Cognitive Sciences, 14*(2), 80–87.

Seth, A. (2021). *Being you: A new science of consciousness.* Dutton.

Seth, A. K., & Friston, K. J. (2016). Active interoceptive inference and the emotional brain. *Philosophical Transactions of the Royal Society B: Biological Sciences, 371*(1708), 20160007.

Slingerland, E. (2014). *Trying not to try: The art and science of spontaneity.* Crown.

Swann, I. (1975). Foreword. In R. F. Piper & L. K. Piper, *Cosmic art.* Hawthorn Books.

Swann, I. (1991). *Everybody's guide to natural ESP: Unlocking the extrasensory power of your mind.* Jeremy P. Tarcher.

Swann, I. (1993). *Your Nostradamus factor: Accessing your innate ability to see into the future.* Fireside Books.

Swann, I. (1996a, September 12). *New scientific discoveries regarding the existence of certain psi faculties* (Reworked version of a paper presented March 21, 1994, at the United Nations). Biomind Superpowers. (Original presentation delivered March 21, 1994, for the Society for Enlightenment and Transformation.)

Swann, I. (1996b). *Remote viewing — the real story: The discoveries, the political and technical history, the rise and fall, the saga, and the strange circumstances* [Autobiographical memoir]. Biomind Superpowers.

Swann, I. (1997, December 12). *Contaminants and "noise".* Biomind Superpowers.

Swann, I. (2000). *Secrets of power, Volume I: Individual empowerment vs. the societal panorama of power and depowerment.* Ingo Swann Books.

Swann, I. (2002). *Secrets of power, Volume II: The vitalizing of individual powers.* Ingo Swann Books.

Swann, I. (n.d.). *Loose diagrams* [Unpublished materials]. Ingo Swann Papers, Special Collections, Irvine S. Ingram Library, University of West Georgia.

Teneggi, C., Canzoneri, E., di Pellegrino, G., & Serino, A. (2013). Social modulation of peripersonal space boundaries. *Current Biology, 23*(5), 406–411.

Thompson, E. (2007). *Mind in life: Biology, phenomenology, and the sciences of mind.* Harvard University Press.

Varela, F. J., Thompson, E., & Rosch, E. (1991). *The embodied mind: Cognitive science and human experience.* MIT Press.

Zaccaro, A., et al. (2018). How breath-control can change your life: A systematic review on psychophysiological correlates of slow breathing. *Frontiers in Human Neuroscience, 12,* 353.

THE SERIES
You Are More Than You Think

Book One
What's Already There

Book Two
Where You Sit

Book Three
The Shape of Knowing

Book Four
Above the Noise

Book Five
The Gravity of Reality

Chapter numbers continue across volumes to reflect that the series unfolds as one integrated structure rather than as separate works. Each book stands on its own, but the numbering maintains the progression for readers who move across the entire sequence.

Elly Flippen is the niece of Ingo Swann and the editor of **Why Do We Feel There Is More to Us Than We, or Anyone, Knows About?**, as well as the author of **Conjunction.World.**

Her work is shaped by years of engagement with questions of perception, awareness, and the lived experience of human intelligence beyond habit and assumption.

She invites readers to rely on their own sensing and discernment, recognizing perception not as something to acquire, but as something already active and waiting to be understood.

To learn more about Ingo Swann and his work, visit **www.ingoswann.com.**